Alexander the Great

The Great Leader and Hero of Macedonia

(The Journey of the Macedonian Conqueror Who United East and West)

Steven Dewitt

Published By **Bengion Cosalas**

Steven Dewitt

All Rights Reserved

Alexander the Great: The Great Leader and Hero of Macedonia (The Journey of the Macedonian Conqueror Who United East and West)

ISBN 978-1-7774719-3-4

No part of this guidebook shall be reproduced in any form without permission in writing from the publisher except in the case of brief quotations embodied in critical articles or reviews.

Legal & Disclaimer

The information contained in this book is not designed to replace or take the place of any form of medicine or professional medical advice. The information in this book has been provided for educational & entertainment purposes only.

The information contained in this book has been compiled from sources deemed reliable, and it is accurate to the best of the Author's knowledge; however, the Author cannot guarantee its accuracy and validity and cannot be held liable for any errors or omissions. Changes are periodically made to this book. You must consult your doctor or get professional medical advice before using any of the suggested remedies, techniques, or information in this book.

Upon using the information contained in this book, you agree to hold harmless the Author from and against any damages, costs, and expenses, including any legal fees potentially resulting from the application of any of the information provided by this guide. This disclaimer applies to any damages or injury caused by the use and application, whether directly or indirectly, of any advice or information presented, whether for breach of contract, tort, negligence, personal injury, criminal intent, or under any other cause of action.

You agree to accept all risks of using the information presented inside this book. You need to consult a professional medical practitioner in order to ensure you are both able and healthy enough to participate in this program.

Table Of Contents

Chapter 1: The Making Of Alexander The Great 1

Chapter 2: The Macedonian Court 29

Chapter 3: Entering The Mentorship 53

Chapter 4: The Rise To Power 88

Chapter 5: The Battle Of Granicus 119

Chapter 6: Early Life And Education 138

Chapter 7: The Conquests Begin 145

Chapter 8: The Conquest Of Persia 152

Chapter 9: The Eastern Frontier 161

Chapter 10: Sources And Historiography 176

Chapter 11: Alexander's Enduring Presence 181

Chapter 1: The Making Of Alexander The Great

Born to the king Philip II of Macedon and the Queen Olympias amid the ominous and threatening signs of the future of his fame, Alexander was destined for the glory of God. It wasn't just the conditions of his birth that helped shape Alexander to become one of the most important historical figures of our time It was also the deliberate work of his parents his teachers as well as Alexander himself who created the legendary hero that we have to this day.

Being raised at the court of the king in Pella, Alexander was surrounded by powerful figures and influence. His father was the king Philip II was a well-known general as well as a smart diplomat, who expanded territory of his kingdom by the alliance of conquest and. The queen Olympias is a member of the strong and ferocious Epirote family she was a lady with determination and an eminent mind. She raised her son in the awareness of his ancestry and cultivated his son with a strong faith in his divine destiny. Alexander was a great learner from his father and mother and was particularly taught the value of a solid, centralized control, the artful application of diplomacy in order to reach your goals and, above all, the significance of a decisive approach in the faced with adversity.

The fact is that it wasn't just Alexander's parents that trained him for his eventual position; his instructors were equally important in his development as an intellectual. As a child, Alexander was mentored by many of the most brilliant minds of his Hellenic world. The most well-known of his teachers was, obviously, Aristotle The philosopher who's accomplishments in the field of philosophy would have profound influence on Western philosophy. With the guidance of Aristotle, Alexander was able to develop his ability to think critically and learned about rhetoric and developed an appreciation for science which included the works of a number of innovative scientists within fields such as science, astronomy as well as medicine.

But Alexander's training wasn't limited to the realm of intellectuals. At an early age his exposure to the numerous facets of war as well as statecraft. He was able to accompany his father's military expeditions and experiencing firsthand the challenges of managing a large and varied empire. Alexander learnt to ride and use the weapon of his choice with equal proficiency as the troops of his father and quickly becoming an integral element of the Macedonian army. Alexander's instructors and coaches instilled the young man a love of the fine balance of power and diplomacy in the battlefield the lessons he'd keep for the remainder of his existence.

In all of his battles Alexander showed a clear understanding of the power behind symbolism and a talent had been cultivated since his young time. It was whether it was executing ceremonies of worship in front of his people, or taking on the title of Pharaoh when he ruled Egypt, Alexander knew the significance of winning minds and hearts of the people who he wanted to rule. Through a connection to divine forces, and tapping into the wealth of the culture and traditions of the land which he conquered Alexander made himself not just a mortal. He was an actual god who was infused with a power that transcended all borders of political and cultural.

The essence of Alexander's story was an excellent example of the development of a good leader. However, it wasn't solely his education, family lineage or the connections with powerful figures that led to Alexander the greatest. It was his personality with his intelligence, charisma, his grit, and his unquenchable need for knowledge that pushed Alexander into the levels of power and acclaim. With the knowledge of his teachers as well as the constant loyalty of his army and the strength of his own mythology, Alexander ventured forth from the shores of his home Macedon in order to take on the entire world. He left behind an legacy that inspired people and leaders for generations to be.

Aristotle, the famous educator and philosopher Aristotle was once quoted as saying, "Character cannot be developed in ease and quiet. Only through the experience of trials and suffering can the soul be strengthened, vision cleared, ambition inspired, and success achieved." Alexander's journey was an exemplifying example to this statement--a flawless blend of divine destiny, powerful power, a powerful mind, and an unwavering commitment. These qualities would determine Alexander through the countless challenges and trials that lie ahead of him in his endeavor to conquer and bring the entire world.

Birth and Lineage: The Royal Blood of Alexander

The dawn sun spewed the first of its rays over the city of Pella The capital of the old Macedonian kingdom. Over the years it was believed that the Macedonian ruling class traced their ancestral lineage back to the heroes from Greek mythology, who ruled across the globe, performing heroic feats of courage and valor. One of them was Heracles a powerful demigod, whose ancestry was thought to be inherited through the bloodline from Macedonia's Argead dynasty. Being a part of this powerful and prestigious family, the the young Alexander III of Macedon, then known as Alexander the Great, exuded an air of power and authority that would define his entire life, and inscribe his name into the pages of the past in the form of one of the most formidable conquerors ever seen.

Alexander's birthplace and his the lineage of his parents were crucial to the development of a conqueror. He was the son of powerful Macedonian ruler Philip II, and the imposing Epirote Princess Olympias, Alexander benefited from the fusion of two different bloodlines each with their own rich history and the right to be great. Olympias was a fervent worshiper of Dionysus, the Greek god Dionysus and was believed to descend from the Molossian Neoptolemus family, the royal lineage of and was the eldest child of Achilles his legendary adventures in the Trojan War epitomized the valor and determination of the classic Greek heroes. In the end, as the culmination from these legendary lineages Alexander was a child born with an instinctive sense of fate that could only get enhanced by tales and stories his mother Olympias told of his family's ancestors.

However, his father, the smart and clever Philip II, the astute and cunning King Philip

II, was the sole person to transform the previously obscure kingdom of Macedonia to a superpower in the military and brought in a new period of interregional cooperation. Philip II not only brought together the tense regional lords of Macedonia under his stewardship, as well as forged diplomatic alliances, and took control from the south-western Greek city-states and secured Macedonian dominance over all of Greece. Philip's innovations in military technology revolutionized techniques and strategies used in warfare and set the scene for the distinctive style of battle that's still being studied and replicated by academy of the military. When he was honed in his skills in battle, Alexander absorbed his father's expertise and knowledge of how power works.

Alexander's dual ethnicity was evident by his appearance as well as his mental makeup. Athletic and tall, with his golden hair and the attractive features typical of a

Macedonian He merged the formidable resolve and constant dedication of his father and his fiery passion and unstoppable determination passed on to Alexander through his maternal grandmother. A sharp intellect and a constant fascination with the world attracted the young man from the beginning as well as his hopes of glory and victory were fuelled by the stories of his great-grandparents and expectations imposed on his by the people around him. This fusion of ambition the mind was a formidable force which shaped Alexander into the person that he was to become.

But Alexander's birth and family history does not fully explain the extraordinary accomplishments he achieved as a ruler or military commander. Alexander would need an extraordinary education, a dependable teacher, and an unwavering foundation in the skills of leading. His destiny etched in the bloodline of his parents would not be enough for him to reach the level of authority the man he aspired to - for that, he'd need sharper intellect and keen judgement that can only be gained through a rigorous education.

At the age of a child, Alexander would be entrusted under the guidance of none but the legendary philosopher Aristotle and his unwavering dedication to knowledge and understanding will play an important part in equipping the upcoming King with the understanding and understanding required to reign across his diverse and vast world. In fact, it was by the careful instruction of the eminent teacher Alexander could acquire the mental skills and the conceptual framework required to unleash his potential as a conqueror, not only of the territories but as well as the minds and hearts of the citizens of his upcoming kingdom.

The seeds for greatness were sown within the fertile soil of Alexander's family lineage and beginnings; and in the fire of his studies and the subsequent pursuit of wisdom, they would germinate and blossom into an astonishing show of military skill and political savvy that forever changed the foundations of public domain.

Early Life and Family Dynamics: The Influences of King Philip II and Queen Olympias

Alexander the Great's life as a child was shaped by the distinct personalities of his parents the king Philip II and Queen Olympias. Both were remarkable strong-willed people, and determined to realize their goals and aspirations and shaped their sons to be the effective military commander who he would later eventually become. Because of his familial dynamics, Alexander inherited a unique mix of characteristics that allowed his to lead at the intersection of different cultures - including the ancient Greek, Macedonian, and Near Eastern cultures. In this chapter, we will explore the influence of his parents, and the way in which their distinctiveness contributed to the evolution of his personality.

born to the king Philip II, who was one of the most skilled leaders of the time, Alexander had the privilege of experiencing firsthand the leadership skills of his father and innovative military strategies. The king Philip did well not just in the field of tactic and soldier but also as a diplomat making use of Macedonia's status as a pivot point between the city states of Greece and the massive Persian Empire in his favor. The ambitious king eventually created the conditions for his son's colossal victories by turning Macedonia into a powerful powerhouse which ruled all of the Greek world.

When Alexander was a young boy during his childhood, he was often witness to the military operations of his father and engagements in diplomatic matters, as well as spending his time in the Macedonian court, observing unions formed through marriages and the expanding of the territory of the state. The experiences taught him the intricacies of political life along with his indomitable desire to dominate and conquer his adversaries. The determination of King Philip to increase the territory of Macedonia and increase its power was the motivation to his son's unstoppable desire to succeed.

However, On the other hand, Queen Olympias was a formidable individual and was incredibly devoted to her son, and displaying the aura of mystery and spirituality. Being a descendant of the royal lineage of Epirus and her mother, she felt an intense connection with gods and goddesses. Her influence over Alexander's life gave the boy with a divine sense of character and purpose. Alexander's love for ancient Greek mythology and religion is traceable to his mother who regularly performed ceremonies of worship and follow the customs and traditions of her native country. The devotion she displayed and her faith-based fervor played a crucial part in shaping Alexander's relation to gods and instilling in Alexander the conviction that he had a destiny to achieve excellence.

These connections to God were important throughout Alexander's later years His victories are always set in their contexts of relationship to gods and Greek mythology. This helped to increase his fame and renown before the people he fought alongside and against. The impact of his religious mother made him someone that was not just viewed as an outstanding military strategist and strategist, but also one who was blessed and guided by gods.

The atmosphere of turmoil and tension in the Macedonian court was another important element that determined Alexander's progress. The turbulent relationship between his parents was a sign of Philip being married to multiple women as well as children, and exposed Alexander to the complexities of rivalries within the family and manipulative behavior. Alexander's survival instincts grew stronger and he mastered courtly intrigues with ease regardless of his years of. The training he received in school helped him develop the ability to think strategically and beat the opposition - skills that would later define his performance on the stage as he began the relentless pursuit of victory.

In spite of the family conflict however, it shouldn't be forgotten that the king Philip and queen Olympias took care of Alexander with a lot of admiration and affection. They were aware of his talent and potential to be a great leader as well as the significance for a good education to a potential ruler. In fact, it was their shared determination to ensure the success of their son which led to the decision for Alexander receiving a tutoring session from Aristotle the one of the world's most influential philosophers.

When Alexander became an adult and adolescence, the many complexities of his early years the extraordinary military skills of his father and diplomatic skills and his mother's devotion to God as well as the Macedonian court's political intrigues made him a remarkable human being. In balancing the delicate interplay of family dynamics to figuring out his personal destiny, Alexander set his sights towards the future, getting ready for the challenges in the future.

Alexander the Great's brilliant mind and tenacious spirit were clearly influenced by the intricate world of the conflicting goals of his parents and aspirations. When we trace the steps of the remarkable man, we witness not just the influence the royal blood of his father had in his quest to become a great as well as the unshakeable conviction that was instilled within Alexander from the beginning in the belief that his path to success stretched beyond the boundaries of his tiny kingdom and the knowledge that his impact would resonate all over the globe.

A Warrior's Education: Early Battles and Training

At a young time, it seemed that destiny would be directing Alexander to live a life full of war and conquer. Born to the king Philip II of Macedon and the Queen Olympias in the year 356 BC, Alexander was a descendent of his father's military skills as well as his mother's fiery personality. Their heritage together set the stage for Alexander's legendary warrior training which was developed through a combination of wars from his early years and intense instruction.

Alexander's education in the military began in the early years of his life when he watched his father's battles from a close perspective. He often accompanied his father on missions, Alexander came to understand not just the tactics in war, but also the intricate nuances of diplomacy, negotiations and the skills necessary to sustain the empire. These first experiences made an indelible impression on the prince's young and planted seeds of desire in Alexander's soul.

Additionally, in addition to seeing in person how wars were fought and won, Alexander benefited from the instruction of veteran military leaders. One of them was his father's General Parmenion He taught Alexander about the use of tactical tactics, troop formations and numerical strategies. Under Parmenion the prince Alexander developed his abilities as a commander of cavalry and learned the subtle signals which allowed him to control and keep control of his horses while in the battle.

The art of phalanx, which is arguably the foundation of Macedonian strength is a lesson that was taught to Alexander from an early age. He was educated about the need for unity and trust among soldiers while they constructed an impassable shield, brimming with spears in order to deter offensive from front. With hours of disciplined training and discipline, the prince was able to command his troops and effortlessly directing his phalanx in various configurations using surgical precision.

As the crown prince Alexander was not just a master of the technique of traditional Macedonian combat, but he also had training in various types of combat to make him a more well-rounded warrior. The training he received in martial arts included lessons in wrestling, archery, boxing, as well as the use of diverse weapons like the xyston, which was a form of spear employed in the cavalry charge. The physical skill was enhanced by his inherent tactical capabilities as well as his impressive war-smartness.

It didn't take too time for Alexander's lessons to be tested in the field. On the side of his father the cavalry unit was led by him in the first major combat at only 16 young at the time - the Battle of Chaeronea. In his elite Companion cavalry Alexander made a major impact against the Athenian troops, securing victory to the Macedonians and solidifying his standing as an adept leader and tactician.

Alexander's training in military didn't just consist of interacting with veteran warriors, or taking part in combat. Learning the strategies of legendary warriors, like those of the Theban general Epaminondas as well as Brasidas, the Spartan general Brasidas significantly contributed to shaping the next strategist's capabilities. The influence of these men, along with the father's and grandfather, enabled Alexander to develop his own method of war that later became his famous military campaigns.

In this crucial stage of his military education when Alexander was able to develop the bold and aggressive style which would later become his trademark as a leader. Admiring fast-moving maneuvers as well as daring flanking maneuvers, his strategy were based on taking advantage of small gaps between enemies' lines to take advantage of chances to win quick and decisive wins. This strategy served him effectively throughout his career as a soldier and his battles against the powerful Persian Empire just further illustrate.

The first battles and the intense regimen which Alexander went through helped to shape him into one of the top military minds of all time. But, the education of a soldier does not end there, since there's always something new to discover and master. In the case of Alexander his path towards greatness could take him further afield - an area where he could blend his combat skills alongside intellectual pursuits under the direction of one of the best instructors ever The philosopher Aristotle.

The Impact on Greek Culture: Alexander's Relationship to the Arts and Science

In the time that Alexander the Great set off on his famous conquests Alexander the Great didn't just expanded his realm and expanded his empire, but also set out to propagate Greek culture throughout the territories that he occupied. What exactly was this dissemination of culture and what impact did it have on the young Macedonian King's attitude towards science and the arts in his day?

Alexander's life and reign was greatly shaped by his innate admiration for the arts. Being the protégé of no other than the famous philosophical philosopher Aristotle, Alexander developed a keen understanding and love for literature, music as well as dramatics. When he was fighting combat and battle, the literature never left his side. The work of Homer such as Homer were a favorite within Alexander's soul as did the Iliad the most frequent accompanying companion during his battles. According to legend, Alexander slept on it beneath his mattress, and believed that he was the direct descent from Achilles.

Alexander's reign was characterized by a truly cosmopolitan outlook designed to connect different cultural traditions and put Greek tradition at the center. The courts of the royal court located in Macedonia and Persia witnessed poets, writers and playwrights composing extraordinary pieces that celebrated the achievements of Alexander in addition to paying tribute to the many traditions of their own culture. In addition, Alexander's own art patronage meant that the most talented artists from all over the Hellenistic world, such as sculptors, artists as well as architects were urged to join him in the battlefields of his army and design lasting monuments and works artwork to mark his victories.

Beyond the realms of literature and art, Alexander was a fervent researcher of knowledge in the field of science. The impact from Aristotle on his interest in science is not overstated. the king's young age showed an intense fascination with subjects such as botany, zoology, and geography, all of which were fields which Aristotle himself explored thoroughly. The influence of science could be applied to real-world situations which allowed Alexander to realize the significance of making use of maps and other geographical data available to formulate his strategies for war.

Alexander's relationship to science could be further highlighted through his encouragement and support of science throughout his time of rule. The city he founded in Alexandria located in Egypt is the best illustration of this. Alexandria was soon the city of learning and technological innovation throughout the Hellenistic world. It was the result of the founding of the famous Library of Alexandria and the Museum that housed the largest collections of manuscripts and scrolls from the period, as well as an institution of research that was able to conduct innovative research across fields.

An illustrative example of Alexander's passion to pursue scientific research is his use of the botanist, philosopher, and philosopher, Androsthenes, to study the fauna and flora of India. Together with other scientists Androsthenes recorded and studied the many animal and plant species that were encountered during Alexander's expeditions and shed light on the abundance of ecological resources and ecosystems in the territories that he conquered.

While masked by the mists of time, a tale is revealed of a king who was equally passionate about developing Greek knowledge and culture as it was about conquering all of the globe. While he was not merely a commander and strategist Alexander's deep appreciation and encouragement of the sciences and arts fundamentally determined his policies, having an influence that remains until today.

In the same way that Alexander's quest for knowledge and understanding the world's natural phenomena drove his exploration into new areas, his belief of the supernatural and divine gave him a sense of fate and the purpose for which he was pursuing. While we go deeper into investigating the lifestyle and rule of a man who's ambitions and ambitions transcended his mortal life, the lines between the divine and human and further strengthen the myth which continues to be Alexander The Great.

The connection to Connection with Gods The belief of Alexander in His God-given DestinyAlexander The Great more than an only military genius or an effective ruler, but an individual who believed Alexander was meant to conquer and lead the globe, due to his special relationship with gods. All throughout his life Alexander believed in the fact that gods guided his actions and that he had been given by them the chance to fulfill an important destiny. This belief of the gods was a major factor in determining his choices in his choices, actions, and in the end the empire he built.

A most notable features of Alexander's self-proclaimed divinity was his connection to the god Heracles (also called Hercules to Romans) He considered to be his ancestral father and godly protection. Heracles was the child of Zeus who was the god of the gods so he was a godly family lineage unrivalled by mortals. There was a widespread belief of all members of people of the Macedonian royal family and local population that they came from gods, and had different claims that they had connections to Zeus as well as Poseidon. Alexander made the most of this notion by stressing his ancestry as divine and traced it back to Heracles as well as Achilles the other great mythological hero.

The faith in the divine guidance and protection came out throughout Alexander's life, as well as in his battles. In his victory at the Battle of Issus as an example it was believed by Alexander that gods were actively involved during the fight, leading his actions and guiding his army to a stunning victory over the powerful Persian Empire. Later in his campaigns the belief of Alexander was evident in his attire his body, sporting the lion's head-helmet - an ode to his great-grandfather Heracles to match his appearance with the image of his legendary father.

Chapter 2: The Macedonian Court

Key Political Figures and Their Impact on Alexander's Reign

The Macedonian court under Alexander's rule was a dynamic and complex political setting in which a variety of important figures played crucial role in determining the direction of the empire as well as the persona of its young leader. Although Alexander's mother, queen Olympias as well as his the king's father his king, Philip II, were heavily involved in his early life, the character of Alexander was also profoundly influenced by the numerous notable political personalities who came around Alexander as he built his authority. The court of Alexander was full of experts in the field of strategists, advisors, soldiers, loyal companions and shrewd rivals all of whom contributed to his achievement and the quality of his governing.

One of Alexander's close counsellors and friends, Hephaestion, undeniably had enormous influence on the King's rule. He was a childhood friend, who was later a respected general, Hephaestion remained at Alexander's side during his wars, giving advice and assistance in things both personal and public. The close relationship between them resulted in Hephaestion being a powerful influencer over the monarch; he was a key player in important decisions and was often the listening ear for Alexander's commander.

For matters of the government, Alexander was heavily dependent on his accomplished and skilled adviser, Antipater. In his capacity as the regent of Macedonia when Alexander was off on campaign, Antipater was responsible for overseeing the affairs of the kingdom and maintaining its peace. His skillful handling of conflicts and political turmoil can be seen in the fact that he kept the Macedonian the throne in order during Alexander's lengthy absences. It gave the king of Macedonia confidence in his expansive expansion plans, and not have to worry about power struggles or uprisings within his own country.

One of the most skilled and experienced military commanders at Alexander's court Parmenion played an important function during the Macedonian battles. Parmenion brought a wealth of experience along with strategic insight and solid feet to support Alexander's bold strategies for military. This veteran general played an integral role in numerous victories including that of the Battle of Issus as well as the battles of Tyre and Gaza and helped secure crucial territory gains that would form Alexander's sprawling empire.

It is fascinating that a person who was frequently obscured by the darkness of time, but the influence of his work was felt all through Alexander's rule was Bagoas. A popular choice of Persian ruler Darius III, Bagoas was brought into Alexander's side following the defeat of Persia. The mysterious young man was not only a source of information on the workings inside the Persian court and gained the status of being part of Alexander's inner circle. He became the closest and most trusted friend to Alexander, the Macedonian ruler. Their relationship is a subject of discussion in the field of history, but it is clear that Bagoas had a significant influence on the king's perceptions of Persian society and was instrumental in helping determine the goals of Alexander to integrate conquered areas into a vast empire.

These important political leaders together with others, formed the court of Alexander and helped shape the reign of Alexander. Their strategy, advice and friendship played a role in the young monarch's development as a conqueror, statesman as well as the leader of an empire. The influence of these people Alexander's rule that became a legend and their efforts set the scene for

Alexander's remarkable military genius ability, his diplomatic skills, and an incredibly tragic descent towards a frightful and premature conclusion.

The way Alexander's rule was formed by the most prominent political leaders at the court of his, so was his learning through the philosopher Aristotle make him the mysterious leader he was to be. Like the famous people in his court Aristotle's wisdom and guidance were essential elements in Alexander's pursuit of excellence. The skill of a playwright's writer in expressing the language of ideas, concepts, and human nature would quickly be reflected with his pupils' choices and decisions. An excellent military strategist developed not just in battle, as well as in the school of philosophy. It is with wisdom and experience the ability to use the power in a way that is effective.

The Assassination of King Philip II: A Turning Point for Alexander

The murder of the King Philip II of Macedon in 336 BCE is an important and enigmatic event in the world's history, which forever changed the trajectory that led to Alexander the Great. The event does not only represent a major change for the young prince, but is also a source of uncertainty regarding this conspiracy as well as the degree of Alexander's involvement in killing of his father. Through this prism of intrigue, in the tumult of family and political interplay, that we'll look at this crucial incident.

Philip's assassination occurred during an event that was public, the wedding to his daughter Cleopatra and Alexander I of Epirus. This celebration could be the most unlikely place the Macedonian monarch was anticipating for an attack. As he walked into the city's theater with the royal procession, Pausanias--an esteemed member of his elite bodyguard--approached and fatally stabbed him. In spite of security precautions the killer of Philip was able to flee until he was snatched and then killed by the other bodyguards. The manner, timing and the people involved in the killing had dramatic implications throughout the world of antiquity and had far greater significance in Alexander's life than anyone could initially imagine.

The murder not only snuffed out the powerful and ambitious monarch from the local stage and pushed the 20-year-old Alexander into the position of immense power. With the threat of his father's death that was looming over him and looming over him, Alexander wasted no time to consolidate his power. The queen's mother was Queen Olympias also acted rapidly to utilize her influence as well as resources to secure the succession rights of her son. The demise of Philip was as quick as it was shocking, and ultimately it set in motion the machine of empire which was to eventually extend beyond Egypt towards the Indus River.

What was the reason why Pausanias committed an act so blatantly, for the rest of his life sealing his own destiny? An investigation into the murder of Philip uncovers a complicated series of betrayals, motivations as well as revenge. Some theories suggest that Pausanias was once able to save Philip's life during battle and was then subsequently beaten by Attalus who was a superior officer. According to some reports, Philip did not believe in justice for Pausanias in spite of his alliance with Attalus which led to an intense desire to retaliate.

In this setting that rumors about Alexander and Olympias participation emerge. Some contemporary sources suggest Olympias had orchestrated the murder in order to repay the wrongs she had that she suffered and to clear the possibility of her son's succession Some sources claim Alexander may have played an active role too. It is possible that he was motivated by his shaky situation in his father's family and the conflicting relationships with his stepmother Alexander might have viewed his father's demise as the sole way to ensure his future. In the end, the amount the extent of Alexander or Olympias' role in the saga remains elusive however, their quick actions after Philip's death suggest particular determination to take advantage of the chance provided.

The execution of the king Philip II not only served as a turning point in the life of Alexander as well as the Macedonian empire in general. Alexander's inauguration as a King would result in important military campaigns as well as the establishment of cities that were Greek in origin, and intercultural integration across the vast regions that he took on. Alexander's reign began a fascinating period of explosive expansion and unmatched cultural exchange, which will cement his reputation as Alexander the great. However, the shadows of his father's murder as well as the lingering questions about the incident would keep him in the dark throughout his meteoric ascendancy and influence his complicated relationship with friends, family as well as with the political world.

While we continue exploring Alexander's life as we explore his life, we're reminded of how crucial this single brutal event was - the death of a powerful monarch through the deceit of an ally whom he trusted. The event not only altered the course of his son but also the course of the entire world, permanently altering the historical and cultural environment. It is still a matter of debate the thorny issues of betrayal, conspiracy and ambition, which are a part of the tragic death of Philip II, the King. Philip II. This is as the mysterious and fascinating character of Alexander sits on the brink of monumentality.

Consolidating Power: Steps Taken by Alexander to Secure the Throne

Alexander became the King of Macedon at the age of just twenty after the murder of his father Philip II, the King Philip II, in 336 BCE. The King of Macedon was a young man. Alexander was on his way towards greatness not just via conquest, but in establishing his authority over a sprawling and constrained area. The actions Alexander made to strengthen his power and regain his throne were meticulous and well-planned but also bold and ingenuous for the sake of ensuring the success of his next initiatives.

The loss of the king Philip II caused King Philip II to leave Alexander with an uneasy and fragile grasp over the throne. Even though he was named as the heir to the throne by the father of his grandfather, Alexander was a target of the opposition of many quarters and not least was his family, especially from his half-brother Arrhidaeus and her mother Olympias. There were others in his Macedonian elite, like Attalus who was the powerful father-in law and the father-in-law of Philip II, also contested Alexander's reign. In a series of swift and brutal acts Alexander quickly dealt with his opponents. Arrhidaeus was killed, allegedly at the command of Olympias while Attalus was executed following being involved in a rebellion in opposition to Alexander's reign.

Another major issue for Alexander was the presence of simmering tensions in the Macedonian kingdom between the urban-centered Greek populace and tribes that were not Greek. In order to address the issue, Alexander adopted a policy that aimed at conciliation and integration and brought the untrustworthy elements in his kingdom to the fold via mediation and unions of marriage. He, for instance, married his daughter to Cleitus the Black, the Illyrian ruler, Cleitus the Black, which was a significant step towards integrating the Illyrians who previously opposed Macedonian rule in his political base.

It was vital that Alexander to maintain the loyalty of the aristocracy since they formed the basis of his his military forces. So, he conferred significant governorships to trusted individuals in his Macedonian elite, like the general of his father's army, Parmenion. In contrast, he maintained an eye on governors and his associates to ensure that they would remain committed under the risk of being punished. In cases where trust faltered, Alexander did not hesitate to act decisively--exemplified by the execution of Cleitus the Black after he insulted the king in a drunken fit.

Alexander's greatest allies during his early days were powerful generals and advisers to the military who had backed his father. In recognition of their significance in his administration Alexander retained and rewarded the most skilled and trustworthy people. The selection of his general father

Antipater as regent for Macedonia an important move taken by Alexander was a sure sign that his kingdom would be kept in check in his absence as Alexander began his wars.

In order to further consolidate his newly established position, Alexander launched a massive public relations campaign throughout the entire kingdom. He presented himself as the king of liberation of Greek cities located in Asia Minor, even visiting the Oracle of Delphi to obtain an official blessing from God for his imminent fight to defeat the Persians. He was declared to be the legitimate leader by the Oracle and was subsequently endorsed by the public of his authority that further increased his credibility.

When Alexander began his most arduous campaign and set off in his pursuit of Egypt and Asia His power and influence in the home and out to grow. These victories did not just expand his territory but were also an ultimate tool to demonstrate the strength and power of his army by bringing both his the opposition from both sides into surrender.

So, Alexander's journey to getting his throne secured was characterized with a deft blend of violence, diplomacy and advocacy. A masterful consolidation of power in his first rule eventually provided the firm basis upon which to build his campaign for dominance over the entire world. The supreme throne of Macedon with his paws, Alexander the Great knew the limits of his power.

When the young king began his quest to conquer the globe, his campaigns will be remembered in their enormity but also the effect they could have in the blending of different civilisations and cultures. The immense influence and vast impact of Alexander's brilliant campaign, which began from his first steps into Asian ground, is a story that will be the defining factor of Alexander's incredible history.

The Launch of Alexander's Conquest: A Prelude to Greatness

The sun's light danced on the sky as an unassuming young man, dressed in armour and decorated with a king's symbol was preparing his cavalry, infantry and war elephants to embark on the journey that would forever alter the course of human history. They had no idea that their long and arduous journey led to some crucial historical battles for the human race Their names were have been immortalized in the pages of historical records alongside the name of Alexander III of Macedon who was who was also referred to as Alexander The Great.

Alexander's triumphs would not be accomplished without the base established by his father the King Philip II of Macedon. An outstanding leader and strategist in his individuality, Philip had transformed the Macedonian army, and secured the trust of Greek cities under his rule. After his death in the year 336 BCE Alexander, the young Alexander was given the title of leader and immediately started to establish his authority with the deliberate and severe suppressions of the revolts that erupted within the Greek cities. Then he began the long and arduous mission to take on the powerful Persian Empire.

Alexander's ascendancy to the top of the ladder was not just a result by his military skills; rather, his innate ability to think and his cultural sensibilities as one of the students of philosopher Aristotle and his philosophy of life, gave him the required tools for navigating the complicated terrain of East-West during his victories. Alexander was aware of the power of the public sphere and propagandists of the time, frequently portraying his self as a liberator, offering Greek civilisation and culture to the barbarians of the East as well as taking on and accepting certain aspects of their culture and customs.

There is a popular saying that luck favors the brave as it was in 334 BCE Alexander made his way across the Hellespont Strait and entered Asia Minor - the gateway into the Persian Empire as well as the beginning of numerous important milestones of his epic eastern march. The impressive thing is that his army comprised a tiny number of 4000 soldiers - an indication to his unshakeable determination, arousing charisma and his fervent devotion of all the forces that joined his campaign.

The early victories, like those in Issus and the Granicus River and Issus, demonstrated Alexander's innate ability to exploit landscapes, using the versatile and extremely deadly Macedonian phalanx, as well as taking advantage of opportune times. These victories didn't just solidify his standing as a powerful and skilled warrior, but was also swiftly smashed down Persian resistance, which allowed the conquer of large areas without difficulty. Within only ten years Alexander was able to expand his empire until all the reaches of the world known to us and include Egypt, Anatolia, Persia as well as some parts of India with the trail of destruction, the conquest of lands, as well as cultural exchange to follow.

While it was an ambitious and groundbreaking military operation The Alexander's victory could also be a precursor to an even greater, deeper lasting impact upon the entire world. Alexander's vast, enthralling travels enabled exchange of ideas, theories, and practices across the East as well as the West which ultimately connected different cultures into an amazing tapestry that couldn't have been imagined. A master of painting who masterfully layers depths into his paintings, Alexander changed the course of time with each stroke of his paintbrush in creating an eclectic lasting legacy that inspires people around the globe today.

While Alexander was standing on the shores of Hellespont and gazed at the vast and mysterious land that was beckoning him It is unlikely that he would have imagined the magnitude of the accomplishments he was destined to achieve. A myriad of lessons that he was taught as an apprentice of eminent Aristotle was to influence his reign along with his friends as well as the distinctive philosophical debate that fueled his daring initiatives. Many years later, we're immersed in their deep connection, pondering the unbreakable relationship between excellence and formation of one's own mental faculties.

A Royal Education: Aristotle's MentorshipAristotle's mentorship of Alexander is an essential piece of the puzzle that was the intellectual development of the great Macedonian king. The philosopher played an essential part in shaping the thinking of Alexander's princely son by establishing a meticulously designed learning framework that would ultimately influence the character of his philosophy, personality as well as his decision-making skills. Through this time of learning, Alexander acquired the knowledge of skills and knowledge which would prove invaluable in the future battles and ruling.

The unusual mentorship started in the year Aristotle was called by the King Philip II to tutor his young son Alexander. This meeting between these two men must have been an invigorating encounter of top intellectual level - where one of the most famous and successful philosopher of his time, is paired with an enthusiastic, affluent and insightful prince only in his teenage years. This was a match that was bound to have lasting and profound impacts not just on the prince's young age but on the world will one day be shaped by him.

Aristotle opened a store in Mieza which was a tiny town close to Macedonia. Macedonian capital. He established an environment of learning that was serene, similar to the Academy that was founded by his teacher, Plato. According to the biographers of old The lush greenery surrounded the walls encased in ivy at Mieza's School of Mieza which was where Aristotle and Alexander thought and studied and cultivated their amazing friendship. The school provided a setting that encouraged the development of intellect and enabled the prince to grasp the intricate world that was outside of his kingdom.

Alexander's studies cover the areas of expertise required to meet the responsibilities and challenges of the future King and conqueror. Aristotle highlighted the role of rhetoric, philosophy, and political thought in shaping the thoughts of a ruler. The philosopher educated his student how important it was to use logic and reasoning, as well as it is essential to make intelligent, equitable informed, and well-founded decisions. In addition, Aristotle provided the prince with the basic principles of ethics and morality that are essential for good direction.

Aristotle assured Alexander's education was more than just philosophical reflection It extended into areas of strategy for military and the science of knowledge. The young Alexander studied combat arts, as well as various strategies to combat, along with meteorology, geography, as well as natural sciences. These were the essential skills for any future conqueror and gave him an understanding of the globe he wanted to take on.

The relationship between Aristotle and Alexander did not just exist as an official mentor-student partnership. The philosopher earned the Macedonian prince's trust, and changed into a close friend that formed a deeply-rooted bond that would remain influential to Alexander until he was elevated his throne. The enmity between these two people through this mentoring relationship transcends the boundaries of the boundaries of curriculum and formulas, shaking the very world that they shared.

Alexander's Aristotle's wisdom was echoed throughout his mind and heart, reflected with wisdom in each major choice that he made during his time in power. Alexander was a man who valued intelligence and understanding over desire and power, as evidenced by his city-planning as well as his cultural integration projects and patronage for libraries. Alexander's leadership vision and ingenuous strategies were, no doubt an outcome of his academic and philosophical training under the guidance of Aristotle.

In the same way as all wonderful things, the era of mentoring of Alexander and Aristotle was to close. The passing of Philip II was the catalyst that brought the new ruler to the crown and forced him to accept the throne of the king.

Chapter 3: Entering The Mentorship

Alexander's Early Education and Meeting Aristotle

When he was just 13years old, young Alexander was handed over to the supervision by one of the top intellectuals of his time that was the philosopher Aristotle. Prior to this epic meeting, Alexander had received basic instruction from his primary teacher, Leonidas. It was however this momentous meeting that went into shaping the mind of his worldview, as well as his military skills of the upcoming victor. It's worthwhile to study how this amazing mentoring relationship came to be and the way it influenced the evolution of the young Alexander into the powerful leader that he was to become.

The historians have two theories regarding the relationship between Alexander and Aristotle or Alexander's father Philip II, the king Philip II, understood that it was important to provide his son with a highly respected education. Or perhaps this relationship came about as a outcome of God's will. No matter what the explanation the union was valuable for both teacher and student, since they learned from and influenced one another. The convergence of the person who was later to be known as "The Philosopher" and the boy later referred to by the name of "The Great" was nothing other than extraordinary.

The school of Aristotle's instruction began at the tranquil, serene area at Mieza, the School in Mieza. In this school, Alexander would immerse himself not just in the study of philosophy as well as engage in various other fields like political rhetoric, linguistics as well as the humanities. The holistic approach to study provided Alexander with an intellectual basis which would be used later to guide the military strategy he employed as well as his attitude towards defeated people, as well as the policy he followed throughout his reign.

The importance of the study of philosophy to develop Alexander's intellect cannot be understated however, it was not the only field of study that Aristotle imparted to his student. Aristotle was a multi-faceted polymath who Aristotle was able to impart to Alexander a sophisticated understanding of many fields like military and scientific understanding. The diverse knowledge he acquired provided Alexander with the innate and strategic skills which later secured victory on the battlefield and strengthen his devotion to his soldiers and allow him to efficiently manage the affairs of his civil massive and fast-growing empire.

While Alexander was absorbing the rich knowledge imparted by Aristotle The teacher-student relationship was able to transcend its old boundaries, because a friendship bond and respect for each other developed. The two Alexander and his teacher changed the course of their respective lives as well as the trajectory of historical events. Aristotle brought out in his student an interest in knowledge as well as determination to achieve excellence, principles that would be the foundation for every one of Alexander's greatest endeavors. However, his devotion to Aristotle inspired him to donate the wealth he had accumulated to Aristotle's work, supplying our world with an enlightening collection of wisdom that is still inspiring students even to today.

Yet, the pupil would eventually surpass the teacher. In the course of time, Alexander determined to create his own way His rapid victories and a vast empire started to expand beyond the boundaries of his teacher's view. In addition, it is believed that Alexander's renewed curiosity about the various culture and people he met in the East resulted in a change regarding his leadership style and government from his strict Greek background. The way they interacted might have changed over years, but the influence of the teachings of Aristotle upon Alexander the Great cannot be diluted.

The underlying principle of relationship of mentorship among Alexander as well as Aristotle was the discussion of ideas as well as the growth of an always-searching mind that was never stymied by uncertainty. Aristotle's quest for knowledge combined with Alexander's unstoppable desire to succeed, encouraged the young man to be more ambitious than the previous rulers. The boy king was getting ready to leave the safety of his kingdom, and outside the limits of his mentor's guiding hand and, in turn determined to impart to people around the globe the value of the knowledge he'd acquired. It was not known to Alexander as well as his teacher in the moment the fruitful collaboration changed the face of the planet and lay the basis to an Hellenistic Age and etching the relationship between these two brilliant minds forever into the saga of time.

The School of Mieza: Aristotle's Unique Teaching Environment

It was the School of Mieza, nestled amid a lush, natural environment, was a perfect setting that Aristotle could impart his extensive expertise to a select number of students, which included Alexander, the prince's son. Alexander. The unique, inspiring setting played a key role in shaping the future leaders of the future and, particularly, in preparing Alexander to be the great leader to come.

Plato's academy is frequently considered to be the pinnacle of the ancient Greek education. Yet, the extraordinary mixture of philosophy, nature and academics that can be found in Mieza's School of Mieza merits the same praise. It is located in the region of Macedon located near to the palace of Pella the school was picked by the king Philip II for his son's educational needs, drawing upon beautiful landscapes in order in order to build a truly distinctive and imposing school.

The natural beauty of Mieza Particularly the Nymphaeum which was a sanctuary devoted to the Nymphs, created the ideal setting for Aristotle's guidance. The heart of the Nymphaeum was a beautiful gardens strewn with lush flora and tranquil water sources as well as comfortable caves. These caves were filled with philosophical inscriptions which the famous philosopher Aristotle was able to impart his knowledge to his students, which included Alexander, the next king. Because Aristotle himself believed that there was an entanglement between human nature and the intellect of a person and the natural environment in Mieza is perfectly suited to help Alexander develop his mind.

The educational curriculum of the school of Mieza was specifically designed by Aristotle to provide a complete and holistic education experience. Concentrating on areas including philosophy, political as well as ethics and sciences of nature, Aristotle exposed Alexander to innovative theories and revolutionary ideas which later had profound influence on his views and his actions. The nature-rich setting as well as the custom-designed curriculum enabled Alexander to discover new ways of thought, without social constraints and forming creative methods.

A shining example of the exceptional education that was provided at Mieza was watching students study and write about the natural world. It is not a chance that Aristotle's work about the science of marine living things, Historia Animalium, was created during his time at Mieza. Alexander as well as the other students, would go with their teachers on expeditions to diverse terrains in order to study and observe diverse species. The experiences played an unquestionably important part in Alexander's masterful application of science in the military battles he fought, along with his fascination for nature and his knowledge of the ecosystems that existed in the territories that he defeated.

Apart from the obvious educational benefits in Mieza's surroundings The school also promoted the bond of friendship among its students. Alexander wasn't at the center of the traditional collection of royals and aristocrats. His classmates were selected by the king Philip II, with the aim to create strong bonds of trust and mutual support among these youngsters. His reign would be a testimony to his insight as many of these friends would be key players in Alexander's military activities as well as his administration, forming an elite circle of inner circle members in Macedonia. Macedonian empire.

In conclusion I would say that Mieza's School of Mieza was a exceptional and unique school that embodies the Aristotle's teaching philosophy and approach to learning. The stunning natural environment with a unique curriculum, as well as carefully chosen students Mieza was the perfect atmosphere to stimulate the desire and perseverance of the conqueror in his youth. Within the walls of these groves and caves decorated with philosophical inscriptions below in the harmonies between human understanding and nature in which the developing brain that was Alexander the Great developed, setting the journey to becoming a great. When we embark on this journey through the life of Alexander It is important to be aware of the immense impact Mieza's beautiful setting to shape the king that would go through his life leaving an imprint impression on the world.

Developing a Leader's Mind: The Role of Philosophy, Rhetoric, and Politics in Alexander's Education

The early period in the life of Alexander the Great was shaped not only by the military skills of his father his king, King Philip II of Macedon, as well as the other intellectual influence that formed the prince's thinking. Within these influences, the rhetoric, philosophy, as well as political thought played a major influence on the personality as well as the worldview of the conqueror to come.

Let's first consider the impact of the philosophy. The famous pupil of philosopher Aristotle, Alexander no doubt had to be exposed to a vast variety of philosophical concepts which ranged from metaphysics to ethics. It was this exposure that shaped the mental abilities of his brain, enhancing the ability of him to think more critically, rationally and more deeply. In particular, the emphasis of Aristotle on morality given him a strong belief in ethical responsibility and superiority in the prince's young age. The evidence of this can be seen when he was leader and warrior when he strived to reach the heights not only for him and his family, but also for the people he served. Additionally, his knowledge of different philosophical philosophies like Platonism and Stoicism will have helped to enhance his comprehension of the universe and our environment, and allowed him to use a more complex moral compass when decisions.

The next step is rhetoric. the art that involved the efficient usage of language to persuade and arguments, was essential to any leader who aspired to be throughout the world of ancient times. Aristotle himself was known as a great rhetorician, and it's likely the latter passed on the knowledge he gained on this subject to his king's pupil. In the process, Alexander could have sharpened his oratory skills and was able to motivate, convince, and excite his people as well as his soldiers. It is evident throughout his own life, like the time he rallied exhausted army on the banks the Indus River, urging that they should continue to the east into uncharted territory. By using speech, Alexander managed to convey his enthusiasm and motivate others to join in his great plans for conquering and establishing empires.

Alongside rhetoric and philosophy, the young Alexander's studies included him in the intricate and sometimes dangerous world of the political system. As a child within Macedonia, the Macedonian court, he'd be exposed to the complex web of alliances and rivalries around his. These experiences helped to develop his understanding of diplomacy and the ability to negotiate the shifting terrain of power and political influence in his kingdom and outside its borders. A political education would provide him with valuable knowledge of statecraft, legal system, and the best way to run an expansive and varied world. So it is not surprising, then that Alexander could eventually become an effective diplomat and skilled ruler, as well as having a successful military experience.

It's clear that the evolution of Alexander's thinking was greatly influenced through the diverse influence on his mind that he was subjected to at an early age. In a way that, his strength and bravery he showed during battle were magnified and amplified by the clarity of his brain and wide-ranging perspective of his that resulted from a schooling that was rich in rhetoric, philosophy as well as politics.

As Alexander became more comfortable in his position as a leader, he'd start to establish relationships with the most prominent political leaders of his Macedonian court. They would form the way he portrayed himself, his goals as well as his course during his rule. In the following chapter, we'll explore the nature of the relationships and discuss what their influence was on the history of Alexander the Great.

Beyond Philosophy: Military and Scientific Knowledge for a Future Conqueror

Beyond Philosophy: Military and Scientific Knowledge for a Future Conqueror

In order to understand the origins the life of Alexander the Great the Great, it is essential to dig into the roots of his knowledge of science and warfare. When he was a kid, Alexander absorbed a comprehensive schooling that included not just the ability to master language as well as literature and philosophy, but also included an intense interest in the art of war horsesmanship, horsemanship, as well as sciences. The foundational knowledge provided was the basis upon where Alexander's stimulating approach to controlling his army and reclaiming vast areas was to be born.

Alexander's horsemanship abilities For instance, his horsemanship skills were refined from an early time. The bond he shared to his horse, Bucephalus was well recorded. The ability of the young prince to control the horse showed his uncanny knowledge and love of horsemanship, and later resulted in his excellence in the field of mounted combat. as a king Alexander frequently led his cavalry on battles and was famous for his quick mobilization of troops. This allowed the troops to travel across huge distances in a short time.

Additionally, Alexander's passion for the natural sciences provided its individual insights which contributed to his rapid growth in martial ability. Alexander sought out knowledge not just through philosophical writings, but also by studying the world of nature that was around his. From Herodotus through the works of his teacher Aristotle, Alexander drew inspiration from zoology and botany as well as meteorology. Alexander understood the intrinsic value of the flora and fauna helping to energize his troops and potentially weakening their enemies. Nature elements were instrumental in their role regardless of the usage of elephants in Indian combat or the strategies gained from the local geography throughout his many battles.

The science aspect of Alexander's military achievements also covered other fields of natural sciences. Alexander had a keen interest in the concept of the cosmos and the connection between celestial bodies with Earthly happenings. The interest in this area was ignited by his teachers and intensified by discussions with highly respected scientists such as Callisthenes from Olynthus. This knowledge was later used to influence Alexander's strategies as well as his capacity to predict and understand important occasions. It was stated Alexander believed that Alexander was of the opinion that both his successes as well as his fate were linked to cosmic phenomena.

As he absorbed his knowledge on warfare and science Alexander was also an exemplar of adaptability and creativity. A striking instance of his creative genius during the military war was his battle with Tyre in the year 332 BCE. In the face of an almost impenetrable city Alexander created a unique idea to create a causeway from debris and rubble in order to get into the fortified city on the island. Utilizing the land's natural features and resources available, Alexander orchestrated the construction of the bridge as his army coordinated a simultaneous naval battle. This battle would be recorded in the history books as a testimony of Alexander's capacity to be creative in even extreme conditions.

By exploring Alexander's scientific and military knowledge and scientific knowledge, we get many perspectives of his development as a leader. Alexander's skills in horsemanship science and technology, as well as celestial phenomena helped him understand the nature of war and helped develop his creative, flexible approach to leadership. This is why Alexander earned him the name for Alexander The Great.

Despite his extraordinary skills, Alexander's reign was not with a plethora of challenges and controversy. When we start to look into the muddy waters of his royal bloodline as well as political alliances and unending victories it is a question of how did the child who was educated by Aristotle to the person who is known today as a legendary conqueror? The boy who was brimming by curiosity and awe sought more than just earthly wisdom. To understand his divine perspective and the enduring significance of his tradition, he searched for cosmic answers, and sought to be awestruck by the sky itself.

Personal Bond: The Friendship and Mutual Influence Between Aristotle and Alexander

The remarkable friendship and the mutual influence of Aristotle as well as Alexander the Great are among the most interesting features of their lives. This was a bond that went beyond the standard teacher-student bond because they inspired and influenced their relationship by ways that changed the history of the world.

Since their first meeting it became clear that there was a unique relationship between these two amazing minds. Aristotle is the most well-known philosopher of the time came into Alexander's life during a crucial period in his prince's culture and intellectual growth. Within the quiet environment in the School of Mieza, nestled in the lush forest in Macedonia, Aristotle saw in Alexander an individual with tremendous energy and potential. Alexander, on the other hand, Alexander viewed Aristotle not only as a teacher, but as a teacher who was able to unlock the most profound mysteries of the universe and lift him up beyond the limits of his knowledge and knowledge.

The two of them had a mutual exchange with each one benefiting of the other's skills and perspectives. Aristotle was a constant analyzer of human behavior, gained many things from Alexander's insatiable interest, sporting prowess and his very public temperament. The philosopher who was famously considered that cultivating good qualities was the key to living a happy life, was also able to appreciate the burning ambition and courageous spirit which drove his talented student in the relentless search for excellence.

However, Alexander was deeply influenced by the philosophy and teachings of Aristotle specifically in terms of politics, leadership and morality. The lessons imparted by the teacher enriched Alexander's knowledge and provided his with the theoretical tools necessary to govern a huge and varied empire, and to traverse the treacherous realm of the power of politics. Additionally, the lessons of Aristotle's mentorship gave Alexander an appreciation of science and the arts and played an important influence on his patronage of scientists, artists as well as institutions that encouraged technological and cultural advancement.

A fascinating aspect of their relationship is how it helped pave the way for their remarkable successes. In the case of Aristotle his period with Alexander was a source of an intellectual stimulus as well as economic and intellectual support needed for his wide range of research interests, ranging including metaphysics and ethics to physics and political science. In his time in Mieza where Aristotle wrote one of his most influential work, including Nicomachean Ethics and Politics, which have shaped philosophical thought to this day.

When it comes to Alexander and his close ties with Aristotle made him the ultimate Platonic philosopher-king. He was a scholar and warrior who was able to govern his subjects with great wisdom and wit, resolve conflicts through intelligence, and broaden his sphere of influence with a tactical savvy. Inspiring by the wisdom he acquired from his studies through Aristotle, Alexander successfully led his army in a succession of epic battles that culminated in the defeat of the powerful Persian Empire and helped to create the synergy between Greek and Eastern civilizations that would later be the foundation of the thriving Hellenistic time.

Their relationship, however, had its share of disagreements or controversies. The more Alexander's power and influence increased, he started to think of himself as much far more than merely a human ruler influenced by God's divine will. His beliefs were completely divergent from the Aristotle's philosophies about the virtues of modesty and prudence. Additionally, their relationship was difficult when the nephew of Aristotle, Callisthenes, an historian who accompanied Alexander in his journeys was a target of the conqueror for his increasingly obnoxious behavior and his strict adherence to Persian practices.

However the bonds that were formed among Aristotle and Alexander in the peaceful forest of Mieza remains a major pillar for both their lives. It shaped the trajectory of humanity throughout the centuries. While Alexander took on the globe and made an unforgettable impression on the development on three continents Alexander carried the lessons of his revered mentor until the end of his brief but remarkable life. The intellectual successes of Aristotle and ideas, which were always affected by his experiences together with Alexander will profoundly influence Western thinking and act as the foundations of fields that range from philosophy, politics to science and ethics.

In the end, despite any shadow of doubts, their bond transformed and was a definitive evidence of the power of ideas as well as the unbreakable connection of admiration and motivation. In the same way, as Alexander went beyond the borders that were the norm in Macedonia and Aristotle was exploring the infinite possibilities of the mind, their interconnected lives provide a powerful evidence of the catalytic role of great minds in each other's lives as well as the course of events in history.

The Leçons that Shaped the King The Impact of Aristotle's Ideas on Alexander's reignAs a pupil under the guidance of the famous theorist Aristotle, Alexander the Great was exposed to a vast amount of knowledge, which would guide his actions and thinking throughout his entire life. As a king at the age 20 years old, he seamlessly implemented the knowledge gained during his schooling in his reign. This will shape his character, principles as well as the direction of his empire. The purpose of this chapter is to look at the primary teachings of Aristotle that had an immense impact on the king's reign and the ways in which these lessons helped shape the king's character.

One of the main concepts of Aristotle's philosophy was the notion of the "Golden Mean," which explained that the essence of good character is found in finding the ideal balance between extremes. This concept is reflected throughout Alexander's military operations and his political choices in his constant effort to find a compromise between his military strength as well as his diplomatic actions towards the conquered. Alexander's policy of toleration as well as coexistence and collaboration with defeated nations stemmed from his belief in the significance of balancing, something he discovered in the Aristotle's writings.

A further important lesson Alexander gained from his highly respected teacher was the value of thinking critically and taking decisions. Aristotle's logics and syllogisms offered an intellectual foundation which allowed Alexander to think through complex issues and consider different perspectives and develop appropriate strategies to overcome these challenges. The evidence is in the strategic strategy Alexander employed to Persian King Darius III's troops during the Battle of Issus, where Alexander used his skills as an analyst enhanced through Aristotelian logic to analyze the strengths and weaknesses of his adversaries which led to the crucial victory.

Aristotle has also taught Alexander an appreciation for and a love of scientific knowledge, science and the empiricism. In the wake of this love, Alexander set out to not just take over foreign territories, but to gain as much knowledge as he could about their customs, cultures as well as their customs, languages, and traditions. The evidence of this is by his sincere fascination and appreciation towards Persian society as well as his work to adopt diverse Persian traditions in his government. The continuous pursuit of scientific knowledge and research he conducted during his campaigns in the military reflect the passion for science that was instilled into his mind by Aristotle.

Additionally, his understanding of ethics, gained through his education under Aristotle and Aristotle, played an important part in his relationships with his allies as well as conquered enemies alike. Aristotle's ethical framework stressed the pursuit of happiness or eudaimonia by the pursuit of virtues. Alexander attempted to implement the ethical principles of the reign of his father. Although his empire was expanding via military victories but he was still focused on making a harmonious and unified multi-ethnic nation, which was demonstrated through his policies of tolerance to religion and his attempts to promote intermarrying between Macedonians as well as Asians.

Finally, the Aristotlean conviction about the importance of friendship greatly influenced

Alexander's relationship with his most close acquaintances, whom he considered as being his "second self." The deep and long-lasting friendships he had with the Hephaestion family, Craterus, and Ptolemy and others differed from the superficial bonds between rulers and subordinates in the other imperial dynasties. Alexander was extremely fond of these relationships since they formed him, not just as a ruler however, as a person.

In conclusion the teachings of Aristotle included the sciences, philosophy, political ethics and science have had a profound impact in the reign of Alexander. By absorbing the wisdom he gathered from Aristotle, the famous philosopher Alexander was able to apply the principles of balanced thinking and critical thinking, a love of knowledge, ethics in management, and deep bonds to his reign and lifestyle. When the sun goes down over the kingdom he used to rule with a glowing glow on the

Elysian Fields where he now is surrounded by his most trusted supporters and companions His undisputed influence in the world continues to be felt forever, based on the foundations set by the timeless wisdom of Aristotle.

In the next chapter we'll delve more deeply into the tactics of military and the strategic genius that contributed to Alexander's numerous wins in battle. We will examine how Alexander's singular vision and undying determination, along with his unstoppable creativity and awe-inspiring skill, earned him the title "Great" and forever changed the course of human history. As we enter the world of battle and conquers and battles, we will see the seamless integration of the principles of Aristotle as well as the unmatched abilities of a soldier that resulted in battle strategies which would keep generals as well as strategists captivated for years to be.

End of an Era: The Conclusion of Aristotle's Mentorship and the Path Forward for Alexander

When the sun went down on the mountains of Mieza in the Mieza region, Mieza, the School of Aristotle where the famous philosopher passed on his wisdom to Alexander as well as his newest cohorts began a new chapter. In the eyes of Alexander was the close of a period that was intellectually forming and the start of a new chapter in his existence, one where the wisdom and wisdom of Aristotle will be challenged in a most remarkable way when he began his quest to make the history of his time. The brilliant professor and his exemplary student their experience at the conclusion of their collaboration was soon to be heard throughout the globe as the exact ideas of philosophy, politics as well as the world of culture that they studied together became the basis of the new era during Alexander's time.

When Alexander's studies under Aristotle ended you can see how profound the impact the philosophy of Aristotle had left on Alexander's young mind. Under the guidance of Aristotle, Alexander had honed his abilities, honed his the ability to think critically, and cultivated an insatiable interest in the environment around him. Education in astronomy, ethics, medical science, biology, and even politics, provided Alexander with the necessary elements needed to rule an empire. The lessons on morals and virtues including the virtues of courage, wisdom and justice, bolstered the character of Alexander.

Additionally, the great guidance on diplomacy gave ideas for forming alliances as well as managing potential rebellions which could help Alexander very well during his battle against the vast Persian Empire as well as his final conquer of the lands that stretched across Egypt all the way to India. Alexander's capability to masterfully execute his military and diplomatic strategies is a testament to the distinctive mixture of intelligence and courage created by Aristotle's teachings.

The long-lasting friendship by Aristotle and Alexander set the stage for important cultural exchanges that would have influential influences that lasted on the international stage. While Alexander set off on his illustrious voyages, the two men sent letters that reflected the respect and camaraderie among the two men. In spite of their differences, and geographic distance, the connection between them was irreparable. However, the path that was ahead of Alexander was filled with unanticipated problems that eventually tested his strength, character as well as the beliefs and ideals instilled in Alexander by Aristotle within the serene school of Mieza.

The philosophy of philosophers had been crucial in establishing Alexander's character as a leader and ruler. leader. But, that was outside of the confines of his school was going to alter some of the concepts he learned forcing Alexander to change in his own way by adjusting and integrating the lessons of his teacher in the context of different cultures and new experiences that the world he was exposed to. This was the right moment for Alexander to be a young Macedonian to put his knowledge in the real-world aspects of of statecraft as well as the strategic military operation and also to accept the undiscovered, and find his way towards excellence.

When Aristotle was watching his student take the throne to prepare for the challenge of taking on his new world. He could feel a strange mix of trepidation, pride and a sense of hope. It was a feeling of pride knowing the man he taught Alexander the knowledge and tools to conquer the world with confidence; trepidation in recognizing the enormous burden and danger that comes of governing such an empire. Finally, he hoped that his cherished pupil was able to walk on a path that was a balance of power and empathy.

While his teacher washed away his books and said goodbye to him, Alexander stood on the edge of his destiny, equipped with a formidable mind, forged from one of the most brilliant minds ever to be discovered by history. This was the start of the legendary account of Alexander the Great which is now that will live on in the history books of history. It was a tale that found its roots in the unassuming and fertile Aristotle's academy in which the mingling of two brilliant minds and tough spirits created the basis for a sweeping saga that will span across continents and transform the history of our world for ever.

Chapter 4: The Rise To Power

Alexander's Ascension to the Throne

The ascendance of Alexander III of Macedon, popularly referred to as Alexander the Great, to the throne of 336 BCE represented a major turning point in the development of the world's ancient times. Although his remarkable military achievements are usually highlighted, his complicated and intricate politicking strategy that helped him ascend to the throne is frequently overlooked. In addition to his skilled tactical skills, Alexander displayed a unique skill in politics that swiftly and effectively consolidated power in Macedonia which set the tone for a kingdom which would be far more expansive than the boundaries of its Hellenic roots. The study of the splintering of power following the events of his father's death and the roles played by key leaders in the political arena, as well as practical decisions taken by Alexander himself provides an insight into the brain of a prince who was who was poised to rule the globe.

The murder of the king Philip II of Macedon in the summer of 336 BCE which was a time rife in intrigue and controversy set the stage for Alexander's ascendancy to the throne. After his father's passing his aspiring ruler discovered himself facing doubt and potential rivalries but he was able to navigate the complexities of his political environment. His mother and queen Olympias at his side, Alexander cannily outwitted the different factions competing for supremacy at the Macedonian court, including his elder half-brother Arrhidaeus and other commanders like Attalus his half-uncle, who orchestrated the demise of Alexander.

A shrewd grasp of the delicate power balance in the realm, Alexander promptly eliminated these opponents, thereby consolidating his power as well as eradicating any potential rivals in a brutal manner. The swiftness of his actions after the demise of his father, did not just ensure his existence, but also emphasized his unwavering determination to have become the norm during the reign of his father.

Alongside his prudent strategy to eliminate dangers, Alexander's natural ability to judge the political situation was evident when it came to handling the larger Macedonian terrain. In recognition of the fact that he couldn't be a dictator on his own, Alexander fostered alliances with powerful families of aristocratic ancestry that were in control of the realm. Although his father was centralized in the power of his reign, Alexander wisely ceded authority to nobles of the highest rank, and let them to manage their respective regions in exchange for trust and loyalty. However Alexander maintained his control over his own Macedonian army, a structure which would serve as the foundation to his upcoming conquests. This way, Alexander intertwined the interests of the noble class with his own, by leveraging the existing powers structures for his benefit as well as establishing a firm base for his reign.

Recognizing that his authority went beyond the limits that surrounded Macedonia, Alexander employed tactics of diplomacy and strength to deal with his Hellenic neighbours. In the wake of the turmoil that erupted after the assassination of his father, Alexander acted quickly to end the rebellions within the Greek city-states. This helped consolidate his power over the area as well as proving himself as an exemplary governor. Through demonstrating his skills in the field of diplomacy and warrior Alexander earned the trust and respect to the Greeks which ultimately fulfilled the dream of his father to create an all-Hellenic power.

Also, one should be aware of the significant and even prophetic influence of Alexander's schooling under the direction of Aristotle.

Being exposed to the most profound of philosophical tenets of critical thinking and the greatest work of Hellenic culture The young prince's early period was infused by a fervent faith in his fate. Therefore, his quick ascendancy to the throne can be considered a manifestation of his fervent belief of his divine appointment to lead the country. As he navigated the tumultuous political waters that surrounded the Macedonian court with a steadfast faith that was probably instilled through his schooling his ascent to the King's throne is amazing.

The events that led to Alexander's rise his position are equally impressive as the colossal victories which followed. The prince who later became popularly referred to as "the Great," displayed the innate ability to govern which did more than secure his position as the king but also showed hints of big achievements that were to follow. When the seeds of the empire he would build were being planted the mighty Alexander showed the ability of a master to navigate difficult political terrains and establish his power in a firm hold. While we focus on the epic military campaign to cement his name in the history books we should not forget the strength of his political leadership that facilitated Alexander's rise to power, paving the way to build an empire that was unmatched.

The Death of Philip II: A King's Sudden Demise

The abrupt demise of the king of Macedon, Philip II of Macedon, at the age of 336 BC is a significant time in history. sending shockwaves throughout the Hellenic world. It also left behind an unfilled void that would later be fulfilled by his grandson, soon to be legendary Alexander. The murder of a monarch that was executed in such an egregiously open manner, had devastating and profound consequences. Even though it's been nearly two millennia old since that fateful day, the events that led to the demise of Philip II have been shrouded by the shadow of mystery.

Philip II was considered one among the most powerful generals in the military of his day and had a plethora of victories in the military to his name. The plans he had for the near the future were ambitious and included an attack against the powerful Persian Empire as a whole. The question is what might have caused the demise of such a mighty ruler?

The event that changed the course of history occurred in the celebrations for the wedding of his daughter Cleopatra who was married to Alexander I of Epirus. In accordance with tradition, the wedding ceremony was public and the splendor of it highlighted the magnitude of Macedonian strength. It also gave the opportunity to stage an elaborately staged murder. When Philip was entering the theater was accompanied by the pomp and formality that would be expected of an emperor, the killer Pausanias smashed. The blood shed by the dead King was absorbed into the foundation that was the Macedonian kingdom, changing the course of history for ever.

There are a variety of theories about the motives for the murder and about who could had orchestrated the conspiracy. Many suggest that it was political rivals that would have viewed the murder of Philip as an opportunity to gain control of the country for their own. Other have posited an individual perspective and suggest that Pausanias was operating under the influence of revenge or perhaps driven by jealousy and love.

Although many have speculated about it that there was a persistent impression that has been left of the Macedonian court intrigues and partisanship. When one looks at the complex network of connections in Macedonian political life, a complicated tale emerges that is brimming with rivalries, ambitions of betrayal and strength. This is an example of the deceitfulness of political power and the shaky security on which even the most powerful empires be built.

Following the murder, Alexander's quick consolidating of power shows a determination and ruthlessness of the young king probably a product of the harsh environment the which he was raised. After the dust had settled and the sounds of sorrow and shock subsided and a new chapter of historical events was set to take place. The tragic death of legendary Philip II, the King of Spain Philip II laid the foundation for the explosive success of a legend the son of his, Alexander The Great.

Even when we grieve the loss of Philip II, our focus is now directed towards the impending persona that is Alexander himself, an individual who would eventually make a bigger impact throughout history. The terror surrounding his killing was not just a matter of luck, and was a reflection of the world's brutality which shaped the very tenets of Alexander's persona. Perhaps, on the bloody grounds of those days as well did the blood spilled, which made its way into the books of later Macedonian theology.

Paving the Path to Kingship: Eliminating Rivals and Opposition

The ascendance to the throne in the younger Alexander III, after the murder of his father Philip II Philip II, signified the dawn of a brand new period not just in the history books of Macedon however, it also marked the later consolidation and expansion in that of the Greek world. Alexander's rapid success as a ruler did not just result from the events of his father's demise but was also a culmination of a series of carefully planned assassinations the machinations of the political, as well as the military. These actions show a leader who was driven by a ferocious determination as well as a skilled navigating the complex terrain swarming of rivals competing to be the king of the throne. The actions that helped pave Alexander's route to the throne and established his authority reveal a smart and uncompromising young ruler who quickly eliminated opponents and forged key alliances in order to establish his authority.

Alexander's quick reaction after his father's murder is the perfect illustration of his swift and decisive act in the process of securing the supreme throne. According to Greek historian Plutarch, Alexander swiftly established his status as the legitimate monarch by taking his father's funeral vehicle as a symbol of his power as the ruler of Macedonian kingdom. The description of Alexander's risk-taking behavior during times that was racked by emotional and political turmoil established the basis for the steps to follow.

The most important aspect of consolidation was the removal of any potential challengers for the royal throne. Alexander's father was Philip II, the king Philip II, had numerous wives, and consequently many children. The result was the possibility of a myriad of contenders to the Macedonian throne, including half-brothers who Alexander acknowledged posed a serious risk to his reign. Alexander's half-brother Arrhidaeus was, just similar to Alexander was a child of Philip II, the king. Philip II, was considered to be an important political risk. Arrhidaeus was later as the regnal name was Philip III, co-ruled with Alexander could be regarded by a lot of people as a feasible option, causing a division in the Macedonian court among his supporters. Alexander was aware of the threat Arrhidaeus was posing, swiftly arranged to get him killed to end any immediate cause of turmoil and in opposition.

Beyond the family rivalries Alexander was a target of resistance from Greek cities-states as well as foreign powers equally. A number of city-states located in the southern part of

Greece including Thebes and Athens were long-time victims of Philip II's overt encroachment upon their independence, which was even prior to the ascent of Alexander to the throne. The cities of these regions saw the demise of the Macedonian ruler as a chance to be free of the yoke of. Alexander's reaction was quick and uncompromising: he made his way south, accompanied by an army that was strong enough to assert control over these splintering political systems. Thebes was the main target of his fury, having Thebes being razed to the ground. It served as a stern warning to any other city-states that might be tempted by the thought of revolt - a scary decision which nevertheless affirmed Alexander's authority that he had just gained.

In addition, Alexander effectively eliminate opponents and potential adversaries within Macedon and beyond, his capacity to create alliances - and, in turn, stop threats to his early establishment of his power. In recognition of the military and political influence of the numerous Illyrian as well as Thracian tribes that inhabited the areas which border the Macedonian central region, Alexander also embarked on various campaigns across the Balkans. In addition to securing the Balkans from potential threat, he also determined to strengthen his government's legitimacy by building a ring of allies and vassals. The military and political strategy proved Alexander's apprehension and his ability to discern dangers that could be posed, and then swiftly neutralize those threats through alliances or by force.

Many people will be able to remember Alexander as being one of the most admired and skilled commanders of the military. But his way to fame was not only by his military expertise but also due to his formidable ability to govern, his keen comprehension of the many counterparts and enemies against which he faced as well as the speed in which he made actions. When we look at this examination of Alexander's legendary life, we will see an emperor driven by ambition and an exemplary capacity to think strategically, leaving the most room for error and any chance for his adversaries to overthrow his authority. In the process of preparing his grand plan to conquer the Persian Empire One can see the beginnings of an incredibly skilled tactician within the consolidation of this diverse old kingdom. The strategic skills he displayed could be the basis of a ruler who ruled over a lot of the globe as a person who stands big in the pages of the past and is known as Alexander the Great.

Affairing with the Greek City-States through diplomacy and alliances When Alexander the Great took over the throne following his father's murder The foundations for his eventual victories in an expanding empire was not just based on his military skill but equally on his diplomacy. One of the initial hurdles that he had to conquer in his new role as monarch was his allegiance to the Greek city-states which were included in the Macedonian Empire. The Macedonians were a crucial leadership to keep the notoriously divided and unstable Greek city-states unified and in their hands. Alexander was aware that keeping the stability in the home state was vital prior to his famed Eastern conquests. This chapter will examine details about Alexander's diplomatic strategies and alliances that helped ensure maintaining the loyalty of the Greek city-states.

It's important to decipher Alexander's strategy for Greek diplomacy while keeping in mind the long-running rivalry between Macedon as well as the other city states in the time of his father Philip II. Alexander was savvy enough to decide to follow the policy of cooperation and reconciliation, rather than subordination and dominance.

In establishing himself as the legitimate successor to the legacy of his father, Alexander sought the recognition and support from the largest cities-states such as Athens, Corinth, and Sparta. This was achieved by engaging in a number of diplomatic actions, like acknowledging treaties in place and reviving those that had been renewed. He also revived the League of Corinth, an alliance forged by his father, which unified the Greek city-states with the symbol of Greek solidarity and opposition to oppression by the Persian Empire.

Alexander's approach towards city states varied in relation to their strategic significance as well as the degree of discontent with his reign. In one instance, Alexander reached out to Athens in extending clemency as well as giving amnesty to Athenian exiles. However, he also dealt with Thebes with more force, since They had actively rebelled against the king. After entering the city Alexander first sat down to spare the lives of his citizens and allowed amnesty for the government offices. However the subsequent rebelliousness resulted in the brutal execution of Theban officials and the deportation of the city's population. In spite of this, Alexander judiciously limited his revenge to only people who were actively against the regime, but he also offered mercy for those who showed conciliation and accepted. This strategy of balance between the forgiveness of others and his exemplary punishment created an atmosphere of peace and deterrence throughout the Greek world, which secured Alexander's support and allowing him to carry on his oriental battles.

It's important to note the fact that Alexander was not merely relying on diplomacy to ensure for ensuring his Greek city-states' adherence. He complemented his diplomatic endeavors with a tactical military stances and the creation of impressive alliances. In the course of making preparations for the Persian campaign Alexander established a large force in Corinth which effectively maintained an impression of Macedonian influence and strength throughout Greece. In addition, Alexander married his sister Cleopatra to the formidable Macedonian general and nobleman Alexander of Lyncestis which was used as a symbol for unification and as a method to secure power over the state-of-the-city of Epirus that was also his mother Olympias home.

The importance of diplomacy and pragmatic alliances over ruthless suppression was an effective formula for Alexander when dealing with Greek city-states. The policy did not just secure the Macedonian authority over the volatile areas, but also offered solid support for Alexander's subsequent successes. In gaining a better understanding to deal with dispersed range of city-states Alexander could have brought the Greeks into a unified way that was for a long time thought impossible, and served as the foundation of his quest to be immortalized into the history books.

In reality, earning that the Greek city-states' adherence to the Greek city states was only the beginning to Alexander's grand plan. He was a true strategist and strategy, on both the field and in other areas Alexander's ambitions far surpassed his expectations of the Hellenic world and set his sights on the East. The Persian Empire was a massive empire and long-standing foe of the Macedonians as well as the Greeks was the next phase in the pursuit of Alexander's greatness. In the dark of the time, a fresh period of history was about to be recorded as Alexander was preparing his army as well as strategies. The blend of diplomacy and technological innovations in the military, and a pure determination that he displayed with the city states could propel him into the midst of history's records as the most undisputed, unbeatable ruler of the ancient world.

A Unified Macedon: Alexander's Early Reign and Consolidation of Power

After assuming the throne the aftermath of his father's murder, Alexander found himself confronted by the arduous job of consolidating his position within a fractious kingdom. The throne's ascendance in the year 336 BCE did not happen without controversy; the newly-crowned King was confronted with the prospect of opposition within his family and the Macedonian nobles, in addition to the constant threat of a civil war in the Greek cities-states. In an effort to build a unified Macedon which could bear all the weight of his bold plan, Alexander embarked on a broad-ranging campaign which demonstrated his political acumen as well as his power of charisma and diplomacy.

One of the biggest challenges Alexander had to overcome was getting his support from the highly regarded Macedonian noble family. The power structure of the kingdom was based on an intricate balance of loyalty and each faction vying for their share of power and respect. In lieu of attempting to dismantle or reduce these groups, Alexander realized the importance of using their power for the benefit of his own purposes. Alexander swiftly married the most noble women to his respected generals and advisers, creating a web of allegiances interwoven that tied to the highest echelons Macedonian power.

Alexander's strategies also affected the inner politics of his court. He did this with a succession of pardons, appointments and promotions for nobles of a certain rank which demonstrated his piety and secured the trust to those who would be viewed as usurper or pawn. Through bringing his possible adversaries into positions of power within the government of his time and ensuring that they were neutralized, he did not just thwart their ambitions, but frequently directed them toward the achievement of his own objectives.

But, the threat of external enemies was big on the horizon too. The Greek city-states which had suffered in the face of Macedonian yoke, seized upon the uncertainty following the death of Philip, and viewed Alexander as a flimsy and unstable ruler. Similar to what he was doing been in the halls of Pella However, Alexander applied a potent combination of force and diplomacy to bring the various groups to a halt.

In Thebes Alexander's diplomatic efforts attracted a wide audience which led to an immediate reconciliation and the reintegration into Thebes into Macedonian Hegemony. Athens as well was enticed to continue its relationship with the young monarch, though it was amid many murmurs and frustration. In the event that diplomacy did not suffice, Alexander turned to other methods to establish his authority. Illyria, the city state of Illyria is one example. Illyria was adamant against his attempts and began to fight back to fight Macedonian rule. Alexander took action with a stunning display of force, quickly breaking up the revolt and then restoring peace.

But the most significant moment in Alexander's initial consolidating power was the wake of his father's murder which provided a chance to gain power amid chaos. Alexander's quick actions in the aftermath of the event did more than smother the possibility of upstarts retracing their tracks, but also sent an incredibly powerful message to his enemies in the home and out. The murder of his father was a political calamity which shaken the foundations of Macedonian authority, however instead of allowing the crisis to swallow him up, Alexander pivoted it to benefit himself by transforming over the role as a relatively new, inexperienced ruler into a powerful figure that could keep the reigns of a diverse and ever-changing realm.

Alexander's effort to strengthen his position was characterized by a mix of determination with strategic insight and charismatic personal charm. He mastered the turbulent waters of factional politics instilling unity into a country which was at risk of falling into chaos. The Macedon that he took over was divided however, the Macedon that he created in the beginning years was one that was forged new under his leadership as a launching pad for his ambitions, which that he was soon to take into the farthest parts of the globe.

On this basis, Alexander prepared to embark upon his great(est) victory that was the power of Persia and Persia, which up until that point was viewed as an invincible giant dominating all of the Greek world. When he set out to take on the seemingly impervious,

Alexander would put the power of an unification Macedon against its strongest test to date. This would not only determine the fate of his own, but also that of all the generations to follow in his steps, influencing the history of our time like clay under the guidance of a master clay potter.

Unifying the Empire: Alexander's Conquest of Persia

Alexander III of Macedon, often referred to by the name of Alexander the Great, inherited the desire for victory from his father Philip II, King Philip II, a man who's grit and determination had led to the rise of Macedonia from an inferior European strength to a renowned monarchy of the Hellenic world. The young Alexander was not content to be wearing his father's shoes - he would walk through the air with a stride that left an unclean mark on the pages of historical records. When he turned his gaze towards the east, a vast empire sprang up across the sky ready to be taken. The

Persian Empire was at one time a symbol of riches strength, power as well as military strength is now at the edge of a cliff. It was the turn of Alexander to unify his empire by destroying this enormous giant of a country. So, he set off in a war that was to be more bloody, but also more impressive than anything that the world has ever witnessed and was to make him as the sovereign of Macedon as well as the Lord of Asia.

Alexander had an enormous canvas on which to draw however it was his masterful strokes of paint that really revealed the work of art he crafted during his battle. He had acquired a highly-oiled army machine from his father which excelled at the core elements of Greek combat - including the usage of the well-known phalanx arrangement. However, Alexander was a man of vision who exceeded the limits of culture and tradition. At the Battle of Granicus, he demonstrated his strategic genius through feigning a strike on the left side, thus creating a trap to draw the Persian cavalry from their the position. And then, with the swagger and accuracy of a master painter the cavalry was orchestrated to carry out what became the signature of his move: precise diagonal charges at the opponent's flank. It was the result of a stunning victory which proved his superiority over the majority in Asia Minor, setting the foundation for future victories. However, his vision did not come to an end with just one strategy for battle, because it was his belief the necessity of variety in order in order to conquer such an expansive and vast world. So, in Issus He took the riskier and more radical strategy. Instead of basing his strategy on the phalanx. He charged in front of his superior Companion Cavalry, breaking the enemies lines with an astonished strike that forced Persian Darius III to flee. Darius III to flee for his life. Yet again, Alexander's strategic wisdom prevailed, and his empire began to collapse in the midst of his military might.

Even the most skilled artist is required to face the pros and challenges that come with the medium's texture. With the varied landscape in the Persian Empire, with its massive deserts and rugged mountains his skills could be tested to the limit. It was the Siege of Tyre which was a crucial city on the coast, was particularly difficult, since its expert defences, secured by huge walls as well as the natural barrier to the ocean, stood firm against the assault for seven weeks. In no mood to give up his goals, Alexander demonstrated a tenacity which was rewarded with the key to unlocking the city, which was the building of a massive mole which did not just breach the sea, but also penetrated the city's defences. Victory after victory followed, after which Babylon, Susa, and Persepolis were slain by his relentless battle. Alexander displayed an incredible capacity to adjust to the ever-changing circumstances of his victories by adapting his strategy according to the specifics of each battle and mixing his own military expertise alongside the wisdom and experience from the Greeks.

The significance of Alexander's victory can't be understated. both the oriental and western civilizations were brought together one in the uncompromising grasp of Alexander. Alexander's dream of a united empire came to life with the help of not just military strength but also a cultural integration. Alexander sought to bridge different cultures of Greek and Persian people, and set an example through the adoption of Persian practices and encouraging intermarry between conquered tribes as well as his own troops. This fusion led to a change of unimaginable magnitude - called that of the Hellenistic Age - a period when elements from various culture merged in the name of Alexandrian values. In the end, the borders of Alexander's empire spanned across Europe across Asia and encompass thousands of people from a variety of civilizations.

While Alexander's victory over Persia disappears like a glowing sun over the horizon of time, we are remind that brilliance is often abounds under the shadow of the war. Even though his strategies were brutally harsh, his ambitions exceeded the merely motives of imperial ambitions, igniting the flames of a emerging civilization that illuminated the future of generations. Achieved by a strong ruler, the huge empire was an enclave of creativity as well as intellect and exchange. Over all this was Alexander King, a man who was bold enough to think beyond the limits of his era and his legacy was etched into the history books. However, like any masterpiece, the true work of art will never be completed, since the tale of Alexander's victory will continue to unfold, leading him to the mysterious realms of India - - a country filled with stories that have not been told and unexplored problems.

Chapter 5: The Battle Of Granicus

Alexander the Great the Great, a prince of young age with a lot of ambition, always set his sights on the immense regions that comprised the Persian Empire. For him, fighting the Persians was as a quest for personal glory as it was the realization of his father's Philip II's, enduring objectives of conquering and establishing dominance over the East. As the head of the united Greek troops, Alexander embarked on his mission in the early 18th century, and it wasn't long before that the first important conflict took place between Greeks as well as the Persian Empire in the Battle of Granicus.

The Granicus River, located in the northern region in Anatolia (modern-day Turkey), provided a natural buffer between Greek forces as well as the Persian central regions. This was the place where Persian sailors who were under the leadership of Arsames Spithridates as well as Memnon of Rhodes took their presence known against the advance troops under the command of Alexander. The Persians were more experienced and well versed in tactics of war were able to believe they were in an advantage during this war.

But, Alexander had made a thorough examination of the terrain and had a clear understanding of the dangers posed by the crossing of the river. Instead of launching a swift and anticipated assault over the river's muddy bed, Alexander opted for a innovative and bold strategy. Alexander divided his troops in two parts: one stationed near the crossing point, and another group successfully crossed the river from a more unguarded downstream location. The unorthodox approach took Persian commanding officers by surprise because they did not expect to see the Greeks to ford the river in this way.

After Alexander's army were able to cross the Granicus The Persians were compelled to adapt swiftly to the sudden change. The most brutal and violent battle occurred on the banks of the river. several Greek or Persian soldiers tying the other's side. The two sides battled hard however Alexander's brilliance in the tactical arena as well as the sheer ferocity of his men were beginning to shift the balance towards favor of the Greeks in their favor. The war reached an important moment where Alexander himself made a bold charged from the mounted position deep into Persian army, putting himself in peril. The assault shattered the hearts of Persian troops, they were unable to stand the pressure.

The time was when the direct participation of a monarch in the conflict could have caused a stir in the present-day military circles. The risk was that a single moment of misfortune might have become tragic - and could result in a devastating or even irreversible loss to the Greek troops. It is interesting that Alexander took the chance reveals much concerning his temperament, courage and unstoppable desire to win.

As history will have told us, Alexander not only survived his daring act, but also managed to eliminate Spithridates and Rhoesakes who were two of the best Persian commanders, in the battle. The Persians not able to recover from the strategic power at Alexander's river crossing, and the loss of their top commanders in the process, began a quick and chaotic retreat.

The Battle of Granicus, while it was not among the biggest battles during Alexander's wars, provides a earliest and crucial illustration of his extraordinary strategies, his adaptability and extraordinary bravado in battle. These qualities will define the young king's life and helped him win a number of remarkable successes and build an empire that stretched across three continents.

The triumph at Granicus created shock waves throughout the Persian Empire and signaled the rest of the world it was clear that Greeks with the leadership of Alexander were a power to reckon with. The satraps, who misjudged the Greeks in their ability to face their huge and powerful empire, paid the price of their mistaken assumptions. But as stunning as the triumph of Granicus is, his epic tale of conquer was the beginning. He was in for even more challenging challenges that awaited Alexander, when Alexander set his sights on the base that was the Persian Empire and the mighty person who was the one to rule everything Darius III. Darius III.

The Fall of Anatolian Cities: Halicarnassus and Miletus

The demise of Anatolian cities Halicarnassus and Miletus was a pivotal turn within Alexander the Great's battle to defeat the Persian Empire. This pivotal juncture was when the relatively young Macedonian King not only strengthened his authority on the continent of Asia Minor but also aimed to be an ally to the Greek cities that were under Persian rule. The effective besieging of the two cities demonstrated Alexander's ingenuity and innovative strategies and organization skills as well as demonstrating the importance of respect for traditional beliefs and customs of the region.

Halicarnassus located in present-day southwest Turkey is a renowned coastal city, and the capital city of the Persian satrapy known as Caria. Its king, queen Ada who was defeated by her son Pixodarus was in desperate need of Alexander's assistance to regain her reign. Conscient of the favorable geopolitical location that was Halicarnassus, Alexander laid siege on the city in 334 BC by deploying the naval and land forces.

Alexander was confronted by a powerful coalition of Persian forces which was led by the determined orontobates satrap, as well as their proficient mercenary leader, Memnon who was from Rhodes. In addition to this, Halicarnassus was equipped with wall that was high and well-defended. They were built by the great architect Mausolus. Unfazed by the obstacles Alexander's troops systematically walked towards the city with battering rams as well as siege towers.

One of the most interesting tactics used by Alexander during this battle was to employ semi-circular battle formations known as a 'peripolos'. As protection, this form of arrangement protected infantry as well as engineers and allowed they to strike at the walls, without fear of being targeted by the defensive forces. Finally, a breach was made which allowed the Macedonian forces to move into the city. In recognition of the strategic importance in Halicarnassus, Alexander ordered the walls to be rebuilt and secured with his troops.

The decline of Miletus One of the most ancient Ionian Greek cities, soon was followed by Halicarnassus. It was strategically located near the entrance to the Maeander River, Miletus was a mighty maritime city with it's own storied background. It was however in Persian control and had to contend with internal divisions in the political sphere. Alexander was in the city around 334 BC shortly after his triumph at Granicus. Battle of Granicus.

The Battle of Miletus has stood out because of its swift resolution, as well as use of psychological combat. Initially, Alexander chose to block the harbor in the city and cut the city's essential supply as well as reinforcements. This caused the Persians to abandon their fleet of naval vessels in the fear of being entrapped by an increasing Macedonian naval force. After the fleet of the enemy was gone, Alexander dismantled his own navy, choosing instead to pursue an on-ground campaign.

With a stunning display of ability to adapt and military intelligence, Alexander swiftly took advantage of the Persian fleet's departure. In savoring the chance caused by this mishap and overcoming the city's defenses, and seized the city. Similar to other cities he conquered, Alexander opted to respect the customs of his native city, its religious convictions, and the political autonomy showing his pragmatic approach and cultural understanding.

The victory over these two important Anatolian cities showed Alexander's greatness as a strategist and commander as well as an intelligent ruler who appreciated the importance of integrating indigenous cultures. The victories were a major event in his battle in the battle against Persian Empire. They provided an excellent foundation for future advancements into the Persia's core.

The demise of Halicarnassus and Miletus created the conditions for Alexander's next stop the next destination - Egypt. In his march toward the ancient country of the

Nile and the Nile, he was bound to face fresh challenges, and improve his expanding empire by the knowledge and wisdom that came from one greatest civilizations. After he had the Aegean Sea in his grasp The conqueror then was looking south toward the mysterious shores of Egypt as well as the enduring city of Alexandria and would establish as the foundation of the Hellenistic empire.

Battle of Issus: Turning the Tide Against Darius III Battle of Issus: Turning the tide against Darius IIIAlexander the Great's battles in the battle against Persian Empire are celebrated in the past as legendary battles of military and tactical skill. The most significant combats that Alexander fought in his conquest of the Persian Empire was Battle of Issus in 333 BC where Alexander was confronted by Darius III Persian ruler, Darius III, for the first time, in a pitched combat. This battle was a pivotal event in Alexander's war altering the course of events and making an impact over the years to come.

To comprehend the size and significance of this fight in the context of this battle, you must be aware of the larger context which preceded the battle of armies. Following the death of his father Philip II, the king Philip II, was assassinated in 336 BC, Alexander inherited the reign of Macedon and also the role of a conqueror. Alexander immediately began an epic campaign to build an empire that covered three continents. In the meantime, Darius III, successor to the illustrious line of Achaemenid rulers and determined to stop the seemingly insurmountable advances of Alexander and take revenge for the defeats his empire been through.

When the adversaries were preparing for battle as they prepared for battle, the Persians had an edge in terms of numbers, boasting an estimated force of 100,000 men compared to Alexander's 40,000 soldiers.

However Alexander, the Macedonian King had proven the ability of his king to overcome advantages in numbers during battles before.

The autumn of the year 333 BC both armies eventually collided on the shores of the Pinarus River in what is today Turkey. Darius had his soldiers in a fortified and secure position being essentially wedged between the mountains and the river towards their rear. Darius believed this would push Alexander to a narrower front, and thereby negate his strength of combat. The strategic choice he made would eventually result in his demise.

The Macedonian troops sat on the battlefield, in the tried-and-tested the phalanx configuration, with massive infantry in the central area as well as elite cavalry on the wings. The most significant element Alexander's strategy was the creation and use of weaknesses in the lines of attack which is why it was in Issus that he employed the cavalry of his fellow soldiers, under his leadership in order to penetrate an opening within the Persian line to initiate a defeat of the enemy. Alexander's extraordinary personal strength and unrivaled horsemanship inspired his troops to battle with intensity that Persian army had most likely never seen.

The Persian war plan of action was to try and surround Alexander's forces by the cavalry of his left. In order to counter this, Alexander shrewdly stationed light soldiers and peltasts. These utilized their javelins, projectiles, and javelins in a ruthless manner to impede the Persian moving to flank. While chaos was raging across the battlefield and the Macedonian army remained unbroken an indication of their unwavering faith in their king's strategies.

Alexander was not content to simply thwart Darius in Issus He drove him off the field in shameful escape, leaving behind his family as slaves. It was so chaotic for the Persian troops that Darius himself retreated from his chariot and rode his horse in order to escape the wrath of. While doing this the king took his scepter of royal honor which was a symbol for the Achaemenid Empire that passed from one monarch to the next over time--a shocking humiliation for a king who claimed divine rights.

The Battle of Issus was the pivotal moment in the battle between two powerful empires. Alexander's victory shaken the base of the Persian Empire and reinforced his army's faith in the divine plan he had set for him. This required Darius to face an entirely new world where he was unable to more simply overlook his "upstart" Macedonian king or undervalue his military prowess. Alexander's triumph made him one of the top forces throughout the world of ancient times which he would consolidate with victories in the following years until his passing away.

In reminiscing about the crucial significance of in the Battle of Issus in setting the tone of Alexander's battle and defining the course of his campaign, we're struck by the value of leadership that is decisive, sharp awareness, and the tremendous potential of human creativity when faced with seemingly impossible obstacles. A few centuries later, when the city named for him was to become a center for education and a center of knowledge throughout the ancient world, Alexander's military feat in Issus could bring admiration and wonder to the future generations.

Conquering Egypt: Founding Alexandria and the Oracle at Siwa

Alexander the Great's triumph over Egypt was a pivotal change in his military life, since it was not only a sign of his rise as a global force but also demonstrated his ingenuous tactical savvy and a deep understanding of the history and culture. The creation of Alexandria and his famous journey to Siwa, the Oracle of Siwa were both the result of this transformational period in his career, highlighting the closeness he had with Egyptian society and the ideas.

The battle for Egypt started with the year 332 BCE when Alexander was leading his army through the Nile Delta, marking the start of an incredibly fast-paced campaign which culminated with the triumphant entrance of his army to the capital city Memphis. The battle of Memphis had traits of a strategically planned geopolitical decision, keeping the vast reserves of grain in Egypt and riches in mind. However, it also entailed social and psychological effects.

Contrary to his ruthless attack against cities in Persia, Alexander demonstrated remarkable control and compassion towards Egyptian society. Alexander not only ended the Persian tribute system that caused a lot of hardship to the population and portrayed his self as liberator like a pharaoh who resembled the image of the nation's past rulers. The clever political maneuvering of his favored party brought him popularity with the Egyptian people, who accepted his role as their hero in the fight against Persian oppression.

One of Alexander's biggest contribution to Egypt and, perhaps, global history was his founding of Alexandria. The city was situated at the point of the Nile Delta, the city was planned strategically to be an essential trade centre connecting the Mediterranean world to the central regions of Egypt. Alexander himself was in charge of the urban development, taking inspiration from the cities of Greece to design a metropolitan city with a large center avenue with grid-like streets lavish temples, and impressive libraries.

Although Alexandria was later to become the capital of intellectual and cultural life in The Hellenistic global community, it's beginning is a model of Alexander's distinctive strategy for imperial government. Instead of simply dominating conquered nations with force, he sought to build new hubs of culture and commerce by establishing bonds between different nations, using the common bond that was the Hellenic civilisation.

As well as the founding of Alexandria Alexander's trip towards The Oracle of Siwa offered yet another crucial moment of his Egyptian trip. Exploring the depths of the Libyan Desert, he sought advice from the elusive oracle and was adored by the world's ancient times for her prophetic insights. The dangerous journey, brimming by dangers such as tribal conflict and sandstorms was driven by Alexander's firm conviction in the divine nature of his life.

When he reached the oracle's sacred sanctuary, Alexander reputedly received profound confirmation by the Priestess. The exact meaning of the prophecy is still obscure and is not widely known, there is widespread consensus that Alexander received the status of god and the Amun-Zeus's son and further strengthening his godly claim to. The divine mandate resonated with his deep convictions and drove his dream of supremacy over the entire world.

A look at Alexander's victory of Egypt shows the interplay of his military skill along with his political as well as spiritual inclinations, which were accentuated by his immense achievements of establishing Alexandria and establishing a relationship to his Oracle of Siwa. Alexander's time in Egypt left an imprint footprint on the regional history as he sowed seed of Hellenistic civilization while also incorporating aspects from the native Egyptian society.

Chapter 6: Early Life And Education

Alexander the Great's extraordinary adventure began in his childhood years of life and his education. These were a key factor in shaping the person who would eventually take on vast empires and leave a permanent mark in the world of history.

Birth and Lineage

Alexander was born during his summer in 356 BCE in the city of Pella The capital of Macedonia the kingdom that was located in northern the Greek peninsula. The king Philip II and queen Olympias were his parents. The time of his birth, as per legend, was marked by supernatural signs, such as the lightning strike that encouraged the notion that he was fated to achieve greatness. It was a favourable start that laid the foundation for an extraordinary life full of successes.

Tutelage under Aristotle

At a young age Alexander's education was given to the famous philosopher Aristotle. The Aristotle-led young prince received an extensive and balanced training. He was able to study a broad range of subjects including the sciences, literature, philosophy as well as ethics. The teachings of Aristotle instilled the young Alexander the desire to learn as well as critical thinking as well as a desire for knowledge, which could be useful throughout his lifetime.

Philip II's Influence

Alexander's bond with his father the king Philip II, was crucial in his development. Philip was a smart and skilled ruler, saw the potential of his son and encouraged his training in military. Philip was able to provide Alexander with an training in tactics, warfare as well as strategy. His early experience in the military was beneficial when Alexander began his quest to conquer the world.

The Macedonian Court

As a child within an Macedonian courts, Alexander was exposed to the intricate world of politics diplomatism, and courtly living. He was witness to firsthand the struggles for power and alliances that were prevalent in the court of old Macedonia. These lessons would help him navigate through the intricate world of politics he'd face when he became a ruler.

Alexander's education and early life laid the foundation for the enthralling adventure that was to come. Alexander's education under Aristotle as well as influences from his dad Philip II, and his involvement with the Macedonian court gave him the wisdom, experience as well as a world view that allowed him to be one of the world's most powerful leader. In the next sections, we'll explore how the formative years of his life contributed in his rise to the top and also marked the start of his legendary battles.

Rise to Power

Alexander the Great's ascendance to the top was a complicated and multi-faceted event that required the use of both military and political skill. The chapter focuses on the most important events and situations which led Alexander to a place of leadership and authority.

Assassination of Philip II

In the year 336 BCE Tragic events occurred in the Macedonian court in 336 BCE when the king Philip II, Alexander's father was killed. The events surrounding the death of Philip remain a mystery but the immediate effect was Alexander's sudden and unexpected rise to the King's throne. When he was just 20 years old, he was the chief of Macedonia and also the commander of its formidable army.

Ascension to the Throne

Alexander's swift rise to the throne met with suspicion and hostility by a portion of the Macedonian the aristocracy. But he acted decisively to secure his place. He sacked potential adversaries and secured the support of important nobles as well as military leaders through military force and diplomacy. The first time he used his the political savvy of his showed his commitment and strategic thought.

Consolidation of Power

Once his national authority was established, Alexander turned his attention towards consolidating Macedonia. Macedonian kingdom. Alexander was faced with numerous challenges within the country which included uprisings, revolts, and rebellions throughout the country. The response was swift and brutal, squelching protests and consolidating his power over Macedonia.

Early Campaigns

Alexander's desire to conquer was clear from the start of his rule. Alexander embarked on a number of battles against tribes and territories, proving his strength as a soldier and growing his influence. The first campaigns gave him valuable combat experience, and also allowed him to gauge the strength of his forces.

The rising of Alexander the Great was distinguished with a mix of military skill and political savvy. The climb to power of the Alexander was quick, fueled by a mix of factors as well as his personal ambition. In the process of consolidating his power over

Macedonia and refined his military abilities He laid the groundwork for the epic wars that would determine his lasting legacy. In the next sections, we'll delve into the victories that helped him become a legend within the history books.

Chapter 7: The Conquests Begin

The scene was set the stage was set, and Alexander the Great was now in charge of Macedonia was prepared to launch the epic wars which would forever mark his name into the history books of time. This chapter examines the first battles of Alexander who marked the beginning of his legendary struggle for an empire.

Crossing the Hellespont

At the time of the year 334 BCE, Alexander crossed the Hellespont which was the narrow strait which divided Europe from Asia Minor, with an force of about 35,000 men. The crossing symbolized the beginning of his ambitious journey to the Persian Empire that was later ruled by the king Darius III. Alexander's bold move was motivated by the need to revenge the past Persian invaders in Greece as well as to achieve his dream of conquering all of the world.

Battle of Granicus

The first of Alexander's first confrontations with Persian forces occurred at the Battle of Granicus during 334 BCE. Confronted by an Persian army led by Satrap (governor) Memnon of Rhodes, Alexander displayed his tactical ability by securing a gruelling victory. The battle established the stage for future conflicts in the future and made Alexander as an outstanding commander in the military.

Siege of Halicarnassus

Alexander's battle during the battle of Asia Minor led to the famous battle of Halicarnassus during 334 to 333 BCE. The city was defended with Persian and Greek soldiers under the direction of queens Ada and Memnon was a major obstacle. Although it was a battle with a strong resistance, and suffering the hardships of war, Alexander eventually captured the city, adding yet another triumph to his long collection of accomplishments.

The Gordian Knot

When Alexander moved further into Asia He came across the mythical Gordian Knot within Phrygia. According to the legend, anyone who can unravel the knot made by the king Gordius could take on Asia. Alexander unfazed by the complicated knot, cut it in half with a sword. The bold move was a symbol the determination he had to reach his objectives by whatever means required.

Alexander's first campaigns were marked by awe-inspiring grit, strategic savvy and an unstoppable determination to achieve his goals. His victories over the Granicus River and the siege of Halicarnassus demonstrated his strength in the military as well as his symbolic action in the Gordian Knot signaled the unwavering determination of his troops. While he continued to push into the very heart of the Persian Empire new obstacles and successes were on the way which set the scene for epic battles and victories that would mark his life.

The Persian Campaign

In the aftermath of crossing the Hellespont and won victories over Asia Minor, Alexander the Great kept on his relentless journey towards the center of the Persian Empire. This chapter examines the key moments and battles that Alexander fought during his Persian campaign, a battle which would define the course of historical events.

Battle of Issus

In the year 333 BCE troops of Alexander and Darius III of Persia and Alexander Darius III of Persia clashed in the battle of Issus. Darius had a large army, whereas Alexander had a less powerful but well-organized and battle-trained Macedonian group. Even though he was outnumbered Alexander utilized ingenuous tactics and personally led his soldiers to victory. Darius was able to flee the battlefield, leaving his family and the treasure to follow. The result of the battle was a pivotal change in the course of war and Alexander's victory brought him into the middle of the Persian Empire.

Siege of Tyre

A single of the more impressive moments of Alexander's campaigns was the battle of Tyre in 332 BCE. Tyre was a formidable isle fortress, with strong defenses and the resistance to it was ferocious. Alexander determined to conquer the island, he created a massive engineering feat, a causeway that connected the mainland with Tyre's island. After seven months of constant war, Tyre fell to the Macedonians and Alexander's unequivocal determination and resiliency to face the most difficult of obstacles.

The Egyptian Interlude

In the year 332 BCE Alexander's battle led Alexander to Egypt in 332 BCE, and there the Egyptians welcomed him as a liberator by Egyptians who were long dissatisfied with Persian rule. Alexander established Alexandria, a city Alexandria and it would eventually develop into a centre for learning and culture throughout the early world. Alexander's victory over Egypt was a significant event that not only expanded his kingdom, but also established his position as a conqueror of the world.

March to Persepolis

In the midst of having Egypt under the control of Alexander, Alexander turned his sights towards the Persian center, and specifically, Persepolis, the magnificent city. Persepolis. After the defeat of Darius III once more, Alexander seized Persepolis and infamously allowed his soldiers to pillage the city. The significance symbolically associated with the act is not to be underestimated because it signified an euphoric victory against the Persian Empire and its riches.

Alexander's Persian campaign was marked by a succession of spectacular victories and tactical actions. The victory over Issus as well as the sack of Tyre and the defeat of Persepolis proved his military savvy and determination. In his unstoppable expansion to the east, a setting was made for his battles against other fierce adversaries as well as the forming of an empire which could span three continents.

Chapter 8: The Conquest Of Persia

While Alexander the Great carried on his relentless march towards the east, he was confronted by the core of the Persian Empire. This chapter examines the crucial events that led to the victory over Persia and a war that changed the historical course.

Fall of Persepolis

The defeat of Persepolis in 330 BC marked an important turning point in Alexander's war. The lavish city, which was which was the capital of the Achaemenid Empire was an emblem of Persian the power of. Alexander's army, who had conquered Darius III once more, Darius III once again, conquered the city. The destruction of the palace of the royal family at Persepolis though hidden in controversy and mystery it remains among the most famous moments from Alexander's battles. It was a symbol of the ending of Persian rule as well as the declaration of Macedonian power.

Bactria and Sogdiana

Alexander's eastward march dragged on into the difficult landscape in Bactria and Sogdiana. These regions which posed formidable opposition to his progress. Alexander was met with a ferocious opposition by local rulers as well as extreme conditions, such as dangerous mountains. But, by combining of diplomatic skill and military power, Alexander gradually subdued these areas, and expanded his power further into Central Asia.

The Indian Campaign

The most exciting stories of Alexander's victory unfolded as he began his Indian campaign in 326 BC. Alexander fought the formidable Indian King, Porus, at the Battle of Hydaspes. Despite the bravery and strategic skills that were displayed by Porus as well as his soldiers, Alexander emerged victorious. This victory represented the northernmost amount of his victories and secured his standing as a tough fighter.

Battle of Hydaspes

The Battle of Hydaspes in 326 BCE was an epic battle with massive dimensions. Alexander's army, including his legendary cavalry companions, were battling Porus as well as his army of war elephants. This war demonstrated Alexander's flexibility and tactical savvy, in the way he devised new strategies in order to take on the formidable Indian elephants. The victory he achieved at Hydaspes is a testimony to the military power of Alexander.

Alexander's triumph over Persia and the rest of Persia was a feat of determination, strategy and management. His capturing of Persepolis and the expansion of his empire to Bactria and India demonstrated his unwavering determination to be a leader and the ability he had to conquer massive obstacles. While he pushed the borders of his empire further east He left an irresistible impression on the world of ancient times and laid the foundation to leave a legacy that would continue for many centuries.

Legacy of Conquest

Alexander The Great's battles altered the geography of the early world with a lasting legacy which echoed throughout the ages. This chapter will explore the long-lasting effect of Alexander's victories as well as administration reforms as well as the spreading of Hellenistic cultural practices.

Alexander's Administrative Reforms

When he conquered vast areas, Alexander faced the challenge of managing and integrating different populations and different cultures within his empire. In order to achieve this, he introduced a number of reforms in the administrative system:

Satrapies Alexander maintained the Persian Satrapies system, and appointed local governors to supervise areas. He also frequently substituted Persian governors with Macedonians or Greeks in order to increase his power.

The Cultural Fusion Alexander was a proponent of intermarrying among his soldiers from Greece and Macedonia as well as the indigenous peoples. The fusion of different cultures was referred to by the name of "Hellenization," aimed to bring about a sense of unification among his various subject.

Language and Coinage: He introduced a currency that was common to all that was silver, the tetradrachm as well as promoted the use Greek as the official language of the Empire. It made it easier to trade and communicate between different areas.

City Funding: Alexander founded numerous cities that bear the name of his father (Alexandria) and served as hubs of culture, administration and commerce. These cities were hubs for spreading Greek culture.

The Spread of Hellenistic Culture

Alexander's defeats had a major influence on the culture that went beyond the administrative changes he implemented:

Cultural exchange: The exchange among Greek, Persian, Egyptian and Indian cultural traditions led to an discussion of ideas across disciplines like the sciences, art, philosophy as well as religion. Artists, scholars and philosophers of different experiences contributed to this academic development.

Library of Alexandria: The city of Alexandria was founded by Alexander was a well-known centre of education, housing the world-renowned Library of Alexandria. The library attracted researchers and scholars all over the world as well as advancing and maintaining knowledge.

Architecture and art: Hellenistic art and architecture that was characterized by realism and splendor, were spread throughout the Empire. Its influence can be seen in the architecture, sculptures, and urban planning.

Philosophy Schools: Philosophical schools like Epicureans, the Stoics and Epicureans were founded within the Hellenistic world, providing a wide range of philosophical views that would shape Western philosophy for centuries.

Marriage and Cultural Exchange

Alexander's marriages and relations were instrumental in encouraging the exchange of cultures:

Wedding Alliances got married many women of various cultures among them Roxana (a Bactrian princess) as well as Stateira (a Persian princess) and promoting harmony across his various subject matter.

Brides for his Generals Alexander advised his generals to emulate his model, leading to an intermarriage practice between Macedonians and noble families from the local area.

Tolerance for local Religions While encouraging Hellenism Alexander was generally tolerant of the religions of his subjects which contributed to the development of syncretism within the religious community throughout the Empire.

The impact of Alexander's conquers was defined by a combination of technological innovations in administration, cultural exchanges, and the expansion of Hellenistic culture. The events have not just left an indelible mark on the history of the world however they also set the stage for the later progress of Western civilisation and cultural exchanges that determined the history of. In the next chapters we'll dig deeper into the long-lasting legacy from Alexander the Great's Empire and look into the complex issues that surround the legacy he left behind.

Chapter 9: The Eastern Frontier

In the course of time, as Alexander the Great kept expanding his empire He faced new obstacles and enemies on the eastern edge that he ruled. The chapter focuses on his journey back to Babylon as well as the causes of his death and following wars that followed among his generals that became also known as The Wars of the Diadochi.

Return to Babylon

After a long period of conquers, Alexander's army had worn out and longing to return the comforts of home. In 324 BCE He took the decisive decision of returning to Babylon which was the center of his kingdom. Returning to Babylon was accompanied with both reflection and celebration. In Babylon his goal was to consolidate his power and make bold plans in the near next time.

The Death of Alexander

In June of 323 BCE At 32 years old, Alexander's death was announced due to mysterious reasons. The cause of his death is the focus of intense discussion and speculation among historians. Certain theories suggest it was due to an illness while other theories claim that it was caused by that it was caused by poisoning or even assassination. No matter what the cause it was the conclusion of a period and put his kingdom in an uncertain state.

Division of the Empire

Alexander's sudden passing left an open power gap, which triggered the possibility of a crisis in succession. There was no clear successor to the throne to his generals, referred to as the Diadochi competed to take supremacy over the empire. This power battle resulted in the dividing of Alexander's huge empire into a number of Hellenistic kingdoms that were each led by his successor. Particularly notable was the Seleucid Empire located in eastern Europe and that of the Ptolemaic Kingdom located in Egypt as well as the Antigonid Kingdom located in Macedonia.

The Wars of the Diadochi

The Wars of the Diadochi, lasting for several years, included a number of alliances, conflicts and betrayals by Alexander's former generals. These wars were motivated by their desire to expand their territory and establish their power. These wars not only defined the boundaries of successor kingdoms, but they also had a profound effects over the wider geopolitical environment that was that Hellenistic world.

Legacy of the Eastern Frontier

The split of Alexander's Empire as well as his Wars of the Diadochi marked an important phase of the post-Alexander period. The empire was fragmented but it was the Hellenistic Kingdoms continued to expand Greek cultural influence throughout the areas they controlled. The legacy left by

Alexander's eastern frontier was a period of political turmoil shifting territorial boundaries, as well as long-lasting cultural exchange.

The chapters to follow in the next chapters, we'll dig deeper into the legacy left by Alexander's descendants, the lasting impact of Hellenistic culture, as well as the way in which his world evolved and shaped the history of our time.

The Man Behind the Legend

Alexander the Great's journey through history was not just defined with his impressive victories as well as his complicated character, motives, as well as his relationships. The chapter focuses on the mysterious Alexander the Great, the man who was behind his legendary image by shedding some light on his life his personal motives, relationships, and the persistent issues surrounding his life.

Alexander's Character and Personality

Alexander's personality was diverse and sometimes contradictions. Alexander was known for his determination, ambition as well as his unwavering self-assurance. His military brilliance as well as tactical savvy were offset with a fiery temper as well as occasionally, insanity. The charismatic leader could bring unwavering loyalty to his men, but the man could also be brutal and a dictator whenever the need arises.

Personal Motivations

The motivation for Alexander's victory remains an issue of contention between historians. Some argue that he was motivated primarily by the desire for glory and power Some believe that he was driven by the ambition to outdo his father who was King Philip II. He wanted to achieve the expectations of his purpose. Alexander's awe of Achilles' heroic actions Achilles and his illustrative portrayal in the poem by Homer "Iliad," also played an important role in shaping his plans.

Relationships and Friendships

Alexander's relationships with his family and friends were crucial in his battles and life. Alexander shared a deep relationship with his former partner and friend, Hephaestion, who accompanied his on several battles. Their bond was deep and lasting, causing many to suggest that it transcended friendship. Some notable people who influenced his life include his teacher, Aristotle, who instilled the boy a fascination with the sciences and learning, as well as his mother Queen Olympias who had a profound an influence on his life in the early years.

Theories on His Death

The reasons for Alexander's demise at 32 are the subject of discussion and mystery. The historians have suggested a variety of theories that include the natural cause, poisoning or illness. There is no definitive answer and adds a sense of mystery at the end to his existence.

Alexander's complicated character, motives as well as personal relationships give an additional dimension to the story of his victories. Although he accomplished amazing feats on the battlefield but his personal struggles and the complex nature of his life make us realize that he wasn't just an historical figure, but also an individual with his individual strengths, weaknesses and goals. In the next chapters we'll continue to explore the long-running debates about Alexander the Great's legacy and life.

Historical Controversies

The life and work of Alexander the Great has been for a long time a topic of inquiry into the history of Alexander and discussion. The chapter will explore several of the most important debates and theories that surround Alexander by highlighting the various opinions and debates that continue to be held between historians and scholars.

Interpretations of Alexander's Actions

One of the most important debates concerning Alexander is the way in which to view the motives and actions of Alexander. Many believe that he was a heroic person who introduced Greek civilization and knowledge to the rest of the world While others denounce Alexander's actions as expressions of imperialism and oppression. There is debate about whether the Greek was a liberator or conqueror is still a topic of debate.

Was He a Hero or a Tyrant?

The issue of whether Alexander is to be celebrated as a hero, or slammed as a tyrant lingers as an issue of debate. Alexander's military accomplishments are frequently recognized, but his strategies that included the destruction of cities as well as the brutal assimilation of conquered tribes are also subject to criticism. The process of evaluating his legacy is weighing both the positive and negative elements of his administration.

There is an Issue of Conquest vs. Imperialism

There is debate among scholars about the extent of Alexander's wars motivated by imperialist ambitions. Many argue that Alexander sought to create a global empire, whereas others argue that his victories were driven by self-esteem and the need to be like mythical heroes. Finding out his motives is a challenge because of the complex nature of his historical documents.

Alexander in Modern Context

Alexander's legacy Alexander was extended to the present day, when his name has served as a symbol of ambition, inspiration as well as sometimes, debate. His name has been used by a variety of political figures and political movements, which makes his name a source of constant curiosity and controversy. The legacy of his conquests continues to inform discussions about power, leadership, and exchange of culture.

Controversies over the historical significance of Alexander the Great are an illustration of the intricate and multifaceted nature that is history. The interpretations of his lives and activities have evolved as time passes, reflecting shifting opinions and perspectives. When we consider these arguments and debates, we get a better appreciation of the importance of Alexander's story and the various ways in how history is perceived and redefined. The chapters to follow the author will explore the influence of Alexander's work across the globe and its relevance to the present.

Alexander's Impact on the World

Alexander the Great's victories did not just alter the course of the world, but also had a significant and lasting impact that has a lasting impact on the course of human history. The chapter focuses on the vast implications of Alexander's activities and the lasting impact of his actions.

Hellenistic Kingdoms

In the aftermath of Alexander's demise, his empire split between his generals. This resulted in the establishment of Hellenistic kingdoms. The kingdoms that were created, such as the Seleucid Empire as well as the Ptolemaic Kingdom and the Antigonid Kingdom and played crucial roles in the dissemination of Greek cultures, languages, and concepts across huge territories. Combining Greek, Persian, Egyptian as well as other civilizations created a vibrant, multi-cultural Hellenistic world.

Scientific and Cultural Advancements

The Hellenistic period was a time of significant progress in a wide range of areas, including philosophical, science and literature. Alexandria was established by Alexander and his sons, was transformed into a place of study thanks to the world-renowned Library of Alexandria, which kept and enriched knowledge of all over the world. Hellenistic scholars contributed to notable advances to the fields of astronomy, maths as well as medicine. Their work helped to establish the basis of Western sciences.

Legacy in Literature and Philosophy

Alexander's story and his conquests influenced many philosophical and literary work. The historian Arrian For instance, published a biographical work on Alexander and philosophical Diogenes of Sinope wrote philosophical dialogues on the subject. Alexander's contributions and the discussions concerning his legacy appear heavily in the writings of philosophers who came later, such as the Stoics as well as the Epicureans.

Influence on Military Strategy

Alexander's strategies and tactics for war have influenced military thinking over the course of many centuries. The use of his mobile, combined arms as well as psychological warfare, set the standard for the future commanders of military. Some of the leaders like Julius Caesar, Napoleon Bonaparte and George S. Patton studied and studied Alexander's military campaigns to get the inspiration.

Cultural Diffusion

Alexander's conquers enabled a vast exchange of knowledge, technology as well as cultures in the territories which he defeated. The expansion of Hellenistic culture, also known as Hellenization, affected art, architecture as well as religion. It left an imprint that lasted on communities that inhabited Asia and the Eastern Mediterranean and Asia.

Legacy in Modern Greece and North Macedonia

Alexander's legacy has particular significance for contemporary Greece as well as North Macedonia. Alexander is revered as a hero of national significance in Greece as well as with monuments and monuments recognizing his accomplishments. In the meantime, debate about the historical and cultural legacy that he left is a subject of debate between Greece as well as North Macedonia, where the city of Skopje declares Alexander as a historical person.

Contemporary Relevance

Alexander's legacy continues to fascinate and motivate people all over all over the globe. The story of Alexander is frequently referenced in discussions about determination, leadership, and the quest for excellence. His enduring fascination of his story and victories is a testimony to the lasting influence he had on time and culture.

Alexander the Great's influence over the world was profound and encompassed science, culture as well as philosophy and strategy. His legacy is evidence of the power of determination, leadership and the unending appeal of an individual that, throughout his short existence, altered the history of our time. In the last sections of the book, we'll examine his lasting impact on art, popular culture, monuments as well as contemporary discussions.

Chapter 10: Sources And Historiography

The research on Alexander the Great depends heavily on documents and sources that preserve the events of his life as well as his victories. The chapter focuses on the main and secondary sources for studying Alexander as well as the challenges to understanding these sources, as well as the latest discoveries and findings that are continuing to provide insight into his legacy in history.

Primary and Secondary Sources

The understanding of Alexander's life and his campaigns is a thorough analysis of secondary and primary sources:

Primarily Sourced: They are contemporaneous or close-to-contemporary writings by people who lived in or just after Alexander's time. Primary sources for this include the writings from Arrian, Plutarch, Curtius Rufus Diodorus Siculus, and the biographer Plutarch. They often rely on the earlier sources and eyewitness stories.

Secondary Sources The term "secondary sources" refers to written by scholars and historians that were written after the Alexander era. They study and reinterpret the sources that are primary to create the story of his activities and his life. Modern historians that have helped us understand the life of Alexander are Robin Lane Fox, Peter Green and N.G.L. Hammond.

Challenges of Historiography

The interpretation of the history of Alexander the Great has its challenges:

Bias and perspective: Ancient historians often had certain biases, and the reports were affected by the social and political background of their day. In the case of Alexander, Roman historians like Curtius Rufus looked at Alexander by looking through the prism to understand Roman imperialism.

There are gaps within The Historical Record: The passage of time and loss of historic documents has left unanswered questions about some aspects of Alexander's story. The motivations and events of certain times remain unclear or subject to the possibility of.

Contradictory accounts The various sources of the ancient past often give conflicting information about similar events, or specifics of Alexander's personal life. Historical historians need to assess the reliability of these sources, and then find a way to reconcile the differences.

Recent Discoveries and Research

Recent discoveries of archaeological artifacts and research advances have brought new perspectives to the research on Alexander:

Archaeological Excavations: In-progress excavations taking place in the areas Alexander conquered such as Egypt, Central Asia, and India and Central Asia, have revealed precious artifacts, as well as knowledge about the different cultures that he came across.

DNA Analysis: Genetic analyses of the remains of ancient times including those found at Alexander's burial site in Egypt offer clues to his lineage as well as the origins for his lineage.

Multidisciplinary approaches: historians as well as archaeologists, Linguists and many other scholars work together in the pursuit of a better knowledge of Alexander's life and his legacy.

Debates and Interpretations

The research on Alexander the Great is an ongoing area, and is subject to constant debates and changing opinions. The scholars continue to investigate the details of his life like his connection to Hephaestion and the extent of his beliefs about religion, as well as the reasons for the time of his death.

When we explore the complexity of historiography as well as sources, we develop more understanding of the challenges and rewards involved in researching the legacy and life of an individual as iconic and mysterious such as Alexander the Great. The final chapters in this book, we'll examine how Alexander's tale is reflected in popular culture, art and in current discussion.

Chapter 11: Alexander's Enduring Presence

The impact that was left by Alexander the Great surpasses the borders of time, and remains awe-inspiring to the minds of millions. The chapter examines Alexander's long-lasting influence on literature, art and popular culture, as well as historical monuments and current discussions as well as how his legacy continues to be alive and pertinent.

Art and Literature

Through time authors and artists are influenced by Alexander's adventures and life. From the earliest Greek sculptures and frescoes, to Renaissance paintings, and even modern-day novels Alexander's tale has served as an abundant source for creative and literary expression. Some notable pieces include"Alexander Romance," a collection of poems and paintings "Alexander Romance," a collection of fanciful tales of his exploits, as well as an epic piece of poetry "Alexander" by the French author Andre Malraux.

Monuments and Memorials

Monuments and memorials devoted to Alexander are scattered throughout across the world. In Greece the Greeks have statues and monuments that recognize his role as a national hero as well as cities across Asia and the Middle East and Asia still have his namesake. The huge statue of equestrian Alexander from Skopje, North Macedonia, is an example from the present of his lasting influence on the public realm and its identity.

Pop Culture and Media

Alexander's tale has also left its mark on pop media. Films such as "Alexander" (2004) and "Alexander the Great" (1956) have brought Alexander's life on the silver screen though the interpretations differ with respect to authenticity to the historical facts. Book, games and documentaries also continue his legacy, assuring that his tale is shared with the next generation.

Contemporary Debates

Alexander the Great remains the subject of debate in current discussions and debates:

National Identity and Nationalism Alexander's national culture and identity remains unresolved within Greece as well as North Macedonia, where historical as well as political concerns are at odds.

Ambition and Leadership: Alexander's style of leadership and his ambitions are often mentioned in discussions with contemporary leaders as well as the historical parallels.

Ethics and Morality His actions, which include destruction of cities as well as the subjugation of conquered populations pose ethical issues regarding the meaning of conquest and the concept of empire.

Inspiration and Education: Alexander's story is frequently mentioned as an inspiration source in personal development in leadership, as well as striving for excellence.

Historical Reassessment

Recent studies have led to an examination of Alexander's life and legacy. The study has revealed the previously ignored aspects of his life goals, motivations, and achievements. Recent advances in archaeology, gene research, and interdisciplinary research continue to shed a new illumination on Alexander's life and his time.

www.ingramcontent.com/pod-product-compliance
Lightning Source LLC
Chambersburg PA
CBHW071439080526
44587CB00014B/1913